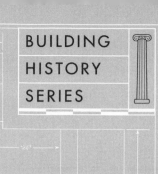

BUILDING
HISTORY
SERIES

THE
TRANSCONTINENTAL
RAILROAD

Titles in the Building History Series Include:

BUILDING
HISTORY
SERIES

THE
TRANSCONTINENTAL
RAILROAD

by Tom Streissguth

Lucent Books, Inc., San Diego, California

Library of Congress Cataloging-in-Publication Data

Streissguth, Thomas, 1958–
　　The transcontinental railroad / by Thomas Streissguth.
　　　　p.　　cm. — (Building history series)
　　Includes bibliographical references and index.
　　Summary: Discusses the history of the transcontinental railroad, including the construction of the Central Pacific, Union Pacific, and other related railroads which joined the east and west
coasts by meeting at Promontory Point, Utah.
　　ISBN 1-56006-564-8 (lib. bdg. : alk. paper)
　　1. Union Pacific Railroad Company—History Juvenile literature.　　2. Central Pacific Railroad Company—History Juvenile literature.　　3. Railroads—United States—History Juvenile
literature.　　[1. Pacific railroads. 2. Railroads—History.]
I. Title.　　II. Series.
　HE2791.U55S77　　2000
　385'.0973—dc21　　　　　　　　　　　　　　　　　　　　99-26335
　　　　　　　　　　　　　　　　　　　　　　　　　　　　　　　CIP

Copyright 2000 by Lucent Books, Inc.
P.O. Box 289011, San Diego, California, 92198-9011

Printed in the U.S.A.

CONTENTS

FOREWORD

Throughout history, as civilizations have evolved and prospered, each has produced unique buildings and architectural styles. Combining the need for both utility and artistic expression, a society's buildings, particularly its large-scale public structures, often reflect the individual character traits that distinguish it from other societies. In a very real sense, then, buildings express a society's values and unique characteristics in tangible form. As scholar Anita Abramovitz comments in her book *People and Spaces*, "Our ways of living and thinking—our habits, needs, fear of enemies, aspirations, materialistic concerns, and religious beliefs—have influenced the kinds of spaces that we build and that later surround and include us."

That specific types and styles of structures constitute an outward expression of the spirit of an individual people or era can be seen in the diverse ways that various societies have built palaces, fortresses, tombs, churches, government buildings, sports arenas, public works, and other such monuments. The ancient Greeks, for instance, were a supremely rational people who originated Western philosophy and science, including the atomic theory and the realization that the earth is a sphere. Their public buildings, epitomized by Athens's magnificent Parthenon temple, were equally rational, emphasizing order, harmony, reason, and above all, restraint.

By contrast, the Romans, who conquered and absorbed the Greek lands, were a highly practical people preoccupied with acquiring and wielding power over others. The Romans greatly admired and readily copied elements of Greek architecture, but modified and adapted them to their own needs. "Roman genius was called into action by the enormous practical needs of a world empire," wrote historian Edith Hamilton. "Rome met them magnificently. Buildings tremendous, indomitable, amphitheaters where eighty thousand could watch a spectacle, baths where three thousand could bathe at the same time."

In medieval Europe, God heavily influenced and motivated the people, and religion permeated all aspects of society, molding people's worldviews and guiding their everyday actions. That spiritual mindset is reflected in the most important medieval structure—the Gothic cathedral—which, in a sense, was a model of heavenly cities. As scholar Anne Fremantle so elegantly phrases it, the cathedrals were "harmonious elevations of stone and glass reaching up to heaven to seek and receive the light [of God]."

Our more secular modern age, in contrast, is driven by the realities of a global economy, advanced technology, and mass communications. Responding to the needs of international trade and the growth of cities housing millions of people, today's builders construct engineering marvels, among them towering skyscrapers of steel and glass, mammoth marine canals, and huge and elaborate rapid transit systems, all of which would have left their ancestors, even the Romans, awestruck.

In examining some of humanity's greatest edifices, Lucent Books' Building History series recognizes this close relationship between a society's historical character and its buildings. Each volume in the series begins with a historical sketch of the people who erected the edifice, exploring their major achievements as well as the beliefs, customs, and societal needs that dictated the variety, functions, and styles of their buildings. A detailed explanation of how the selected structure was conceived, designed, and built, to the extent that this information is known, makes up the majority of the volume.

Each volume in the Lucent Building History series also includes several special features that are useful tools for additional research. A chronology of important dates gives students an overview, at a glance, of the evolution and use of the structure described. Sidebars create a broader context by adding further details on some of the architects, engineers, and construction tools, materials, and methods that made each structure a reality, as well as the social, political, and/or religious leaders and movements that inspired its creation. Useful maps help the reader locate the nations, cities, streets, and individual structures mentioned in the text; and numerous diagrams and pictures illustrate tools and devices that bring to life various stages of construction. Finally, each volume contains two bibliographies, one for student research, the other listing works the author consulted in compiling the book.

Taken as a whole, these volumes, covering diverse ancient and modern structures, constitute not only a valuable research tool, but also a tribute to the human spirit, a fascinating exploration of the dreams, skills, ingenuity, and dogged determination of the great peoples who shaped history.

Important Dates in the Building of the Transcontinental Railroad

Work crews lay track for the transcontinental railroad.

1829
The first English locomotive arrives in the United States.

1845
Asa Whitney first proposes construction of a transcontinental railroad.

1825	1840	1855

1853
Congress authorizes western surveys for a future transcontinental route.

Workers and bystanders celebrate the completion of the project.

1859
Theodore Judah asks the California Assembly to consider financing a transcontinental railroad.

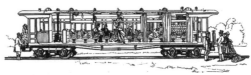

A cross-section of one of the railroad's passenger cars.

1863
The Central Pacific Railroad breaks ground in Sacramento, California.

1867
A Cheyenne war party raids a Union Pacific train at Plum Creek, Nebraska.

1861
The Central Pacific Railway is incorporated.

1868
The Central Pacific reaches the future site of Reno, Nevada.

| 1860 | 1865 | 1870 | 1875 | 1880 |

1869
The Central Pacific sets a record for the most track laid in one day.

1864
Crews lay the Union Pacific's first rail in Omaha, Nebraska.

The Central Pacific begins regular passenger service in California.

The transcontinental railroad is linked at Promontory, Utah.

1862
President Lincoln signs the Pacific Railroad Act.

1860
Theodore Judah sets out to survey a railroad route through the Sierras.

INTRODUCTION

In the early morning of a spring day in 1854, a passenger steamer bound for Central America cast off from a crowded dock in New York Harbor. From the deck of the steamer, Theodore and Anna Judah watched the streets and buildings of the city slip gradually into the distance. They were headed for California and knew they would not see New York or the East again for a long time. They would be traveling for weeks, taking passage on two oceangoing ships and an overland coach through Central America. As soon as they arrived in California's capital of Sacramento, Theodore Judah would take up his assignment to build the Sacramento Valley Railroad, the first railroad west of the Rocky Mountains.

Although railroads now crisscrossed the northeastern states, serving hundreds of small towns and big cities, travel to California was a tougher proposition. Commodore Cornelius Vanderbilt, who owned the steamer carrying the Judahs and their fellow passengers, had developed the quickest route to the west coast. His boats called at the mouth of the San Juan River, on the east coast of Nicaragua, then followed the river to Lake Nicaragua. From the west shore of the lake, Vanderbilt provided coach service to Nicaragua's Pacific coast, where passengers caught another boat for the final leg to San Francisco.

Vanderbilt's route cut two days off the trip from New York to California via the more southerly Isthmus of Panama. Still, as historian Robert West Howard described it,

Overland Routes to California

A SHREWD OPERATOR

The ambitious and devious Cornelius Vanderbilt was one of the first to make a fortune from railroads in the United States. In her book *Passage to Union,* railway historian Sarah H. Gordon describes some of the methods Vanderbilt and his partner, Daniel Drew, used to get their way:

> In addition to arranging passenger schedules and connections to suit their financial interests, both Drew and Vanderbilt became known for their high-handed manipulation of city and state governments for their own ends. The process of acquiring the rights to use stations and routes under the authority of city and state governments was as complex as every other aspect of railroad law at this time. Every boundary crossed brought the railroads into a new legal jurisdiction. What made Vanderbilt and Drew famous was their ability to simplify the process by using financial pressures to force legislatures and city councils into granting them whatever they sought. When the city council of New York, for example, stood in the way of his taking control of the New York and Harlem River Railroad, Vanderbilt rigged three corners on the stock exchange, two of them simultaneously, a feat that called for all the available millions even of the Commodore.

Using sometimes unscrupulous tactics, Cornelius Vanderbilt made a fortune from the railroad.

The idea of national political unity was translated practically into a series of cutthroat schemes by which a small group of nationally known railroad directors virtually declared war on one another to sweep away competition and control as much track mileage as possible. Only when one of these men controlled his own railroad empire, or system, did the ideal of providing quick and dependable travel connections become attractive to him.

The trip took five to six weeks, barring hurricanes and gales in the Atlantic, tropical floods in the San Juan River, mud or rock slides in the Cordillera [Central American mountain ranges], monsoons and fog on the Pacific sail. Ever present, too, was the likelihood of tropical disease, especially the mysterious and deadly yellow fever.[1]

As difficult as the route via Central America might be, the overland route across North America, by stagecoach or wagon train, was even worse: two long, dreary months by rough, dusty trails through endless plains and mountains, past hostile Native Americans and under the threat of blistering heat or biting cold, raging thunderstorms, blizzards, floods, and mountain avalanches.

Theodore Judah realized that someday there would be a better way. Like Vanderbilt, he was a man of energy and vision. After attending the Troy Engineering School of New York, he had designed and built many bridges and railroads in the East— including the Niagara Valley Gorge railroad, which many had believed impossible to build. Why not a railroad across the entire continent, linking New York and California, the Pacific and the Atlantic—a transcontinental railroad? Judah did not yet realize that the most difficult task of all would be overcoming the skepticism of politicians and investors who thought a transcontinental railroad simply could not be done.

The Judahs landed safely at San Francisco, took a twelve-hour steamer ride up the Sacramento River, and settled down in Sacramento. Judah managed to complete the surveys for the twenty-one-mile Sacramento Valley Railroad in just two weeks and see the railroad completed by February 1855. Already, his thoughts and dreams were on the transcontinental railroad. Someday, he was certain, its time would come.

RAISING
STEAM

When Theodore and Anna Judah arrived in Sacramento, self-propelled steam engines had been in existence for about eighty-five years. The first had been built in France by Nicolas Cugnot in 1769. The Englishman William Murdoch built another experimental steam engine in 1784. These "locomotives" worked by heating water within a boiler, then allowing the steam to escape into a cylinder. Under high pressure, the steam pushed a piston rapidly back and forth. The piston turned a complicated system of gears connected to the wheels. With a frightening noise of hissing steam and clattering valves, the first locomotives inched forward, sending people and horses scattering in all directions.

The invention of flanged wheels allowed locomotives to travel on a pair of iron rails. In 1814, George Stephenson invented a set of driving rods that linked locomotive pistons to the wheels. Regular locomotive service began on September 27, 1825, when the steam-driven *Locomotion* made its first run over the Stockton and Darlington line, on a twenty-mile downhill section between Shildon and Stockton Quay in Wales.

In the meantime, adventurers in the United States were exploring the vast, unclaimed western territories inhabited by nomadic tribes of Native Americans. In 1803, President Thomas Jefferson sent Meriwether Lewis and William Clark on an expedition up the Missouri River and across the Rocky Mountains. Jefferson's orders were to search for the Northwest Passage—an all-water route across the continent to the Pacific. In 1804, Lewis and Clark reached the Pacific coast, becoming the first group of whites to cross North America. To Jefferson's disappointment, they also discovered that no all-water route for the journey existed, which meant that a voyage to the Pacific would remain a difficult, dangerous undertaking best suited for adventurers, rather than an easy passage for traders and settlers.

Early Steam Locomotives

Englishman George Stephenson's *Rocket,* built in 1829, featured all of the basic parts of the steam locomotive. The *Rocket* proved that locomotives could be fast, reliable, and relatively inexpensive. It used a double-action steam engine. Small boiler tubes that ran through the boiler produced steam quickly. The hottest and driest steam rose to the steam dome, and from there it was carried through steampipes to the two diagonal cylinders. Each cylinder contained a piston that was attached directly by a drive rod and connecting rod to one of the two drive wheels.

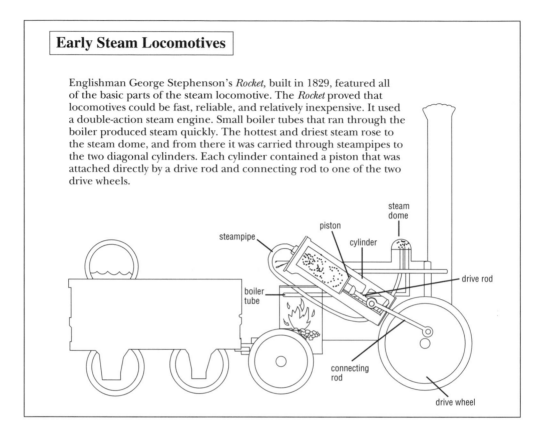

While more expeditions scouted the Rockies and the Pacific coast territory, eastern inventors were copying railroad innovations in England. In 1829, the Delaware and Hudson Canal Company opened a private freight railway at the Carbondale coal mine in Pennsylvania. Soon other U.S. companies were building short-haul railways to do the heavy work of moving goods and raw materials to transports docked at seaports, rivers, and canals.

At this time in Europe and the United States, rivers and canals were still the principal means of transporting goods over long distances. Not all cities and companies were served by waterways, however. Baltimore, for example, was surrounded by a range of hills that made canal building impractical. Fearing an economic decline, a group of local entrepreneurs founded the Baltimore and Ohio railway line in 1829 to carry freight between the city and the towns along the Ohio River. As described by historian Oliver Jensen,

Baltimore was fearful of the competition of New York and her new Erie Canal. Although the city was the starting point for the colorful traffic over the famous National Road, crowded with Concord coaches and Conestoga wagons, farseeing men like Philip Thomas and his brother Evan, who had seen England's new coal-carrying railways, decided that only rails . . . could preserve their competitive position.[2]

It was clear to most people that railroads would soon become the most important means of transportation in the United States. Distances in North America were vast; there were few public road networks to be displaced; and unlike Europe, there were no complex systems of private landholdings to block new construction. Ten years after the first public railway was completed in England, the United States was home to more than half of all the railroad track in the world.

This construction went hand in hand with the country's westward expansion. As new railways were built, settlers were moving beyond the Appalachian Mountains. Someday, many believed, this settlement would reach as far as the Pacific

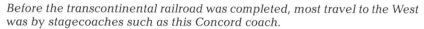

Before the transcontinental railroad was completed, most travel to the West was by stagecoaches such as this Concord coach.

Ocean. The United States would claim and own all of this land, and there was no other country, or Native American nation, able to stop it. One catchy phrase coined in 1845 summed up this vision of America's future: Manifest Destiny.

TRANSCONTINENTAL VISIONS

Theodore Judah was not the first to have the idea for a transcontinental railroad. In 1819, Robert Mills proposed a steam railway to run from the Mississippi valley to the head of the Columbia River in the Oregon Country. In an 1832 edition of *The Emigrant,* an Ann Arbor, Michigan, newspaper, Judge S. W. Dexter proposed a railway to skirt the southern Great Lakes, cross the Missouri River, follow the Platte River, and reach the Pacific by following the Columbia River.

A New York merchant, Asa Whitney, offered to build the transcontinental railroad in 1845. Whitney asked the federal government to help him pay for it by granting him land thirty miles on either side of his route. His plan was to sell the land to cover the costs of construction. The workers who built the railroad, he expected, would settle on these lands, build new towns, and provide freight and passenger traffic to help the railroad turn a profit.

Whitney's idea turned out to be ahead of its time, as public officials still believed that building a transcontinental railroad was impossible. There were enormous distances to cover and hostile Native Americans to deal with. The Great Plains offered very little of the water needed by construction laborers or the wood needed for cross ties and locomotive fuel. As far as anybody knew, the plains held no minerals or coal that might make the land grants worthwhile. Certainly, few people would ever want to settle in this "Great American Desert." The demand for freight and passenger service would never cover the costs of labor and materials, much less earn a profit for anyone foolish enough to invest in such a scheme.

SURVEYING THE WEST

Despite public skepticism toward Whitney's plans, the era of the railroads had begun. Samuel Eliot Morison writes:

> Canals still carried most of the freight in 1850, but the completion of the Hudson River Railroad from New

EARLY PASSENGER SERVICE

Imitating the rigid class structures of Europe, the first public passenger railways were divided into strictly separated classes, as many as four on a single train. Railway historian J. B. Snell, in his book *Early Railways*, describes conditions:

> The first-class passenger was seated in comfort (at a price) from the earliest days, and by the late '30s even had the chance here and there of travelling in a rudimentary sleeping car. Second-class standards varied, but at the very worst this grade of passenger could be sure of a seat of some kind and a roof over his head. Both these amenities were often denied to the wretched third class, who were carried only on sufferance in trucks hitched to any freight train convenient to the railway company. Slowly conditions were improved, both by the pressure of public opinion and because one or two ugly accidents showed that for reasons of safety alone even third-class customers were entitled to better protection.
>
> Sadly enough, most lessons in safety had to be learnt the hard way. One cause of loss of life was the habit of locking people into their compartments, for convenience in seat allocation and ticket control, which was almost universal in Europe. It ceased in France after 1842, when there was a derailment at Meudon on the Chemin de fer de l'Ouest, followed by a fire. Unable to escape from their carriages, several important notables, including the Admiral Dumont d'Urville, and a large number of ordinary travellers were roasted to death.

This advertisement portrays the luxury of early first-class passenger service on railroads.

York to Albany . . . and the Pennsylvania Railroad from Philadelphia to Pittsburgh, caused such an astounding transfer of freight from canals to railroads, particularly in the winter season, as to prove the superiority of rail for

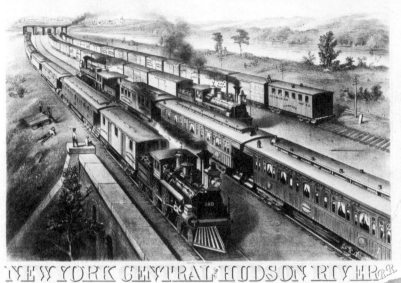

Another advertisement, this time for the New York Central and Hudson River Railroad, promoted the safety and speed of its service.

long-distance hauls, and to suggest that the locomotive was the proper instrument for penetrating the continent.[3]

By the middle of the 1850s, migration and settlement west of the Mississippi was beginning to change attitudes among politicians in Washington. Most no longer ridiculed the idea of a transcontinental railroad. California had joined the Union as a "free" (nonslaveholding) state. Emigrants rode west along the Oregon Trail, risking a dangerous journey by wagon train to reach unclaimed lands on the West Coast. There would be demand for rail service across the Rockies—but where would the line be built?

In 1853, Congress passed a resolution authorizing the dispatch of several parties to explore routes through the Rockies to California. The parties worked out five possibilities, one of which followed the Platte River valley and was dubbed the "Mormon Trail," for the pioneering Mormon settlers who passed that way to Utah. Two other routes passed through southern slaveholding states. The most southerly route started at Fulton, Arkansas, and ended in San Diego. According to the surveys, this "Southern Trail" would be the shortest route and the least expensive to build, costing about $69 million.

Choosing the southern route would be practical and cheap. But the proposed railroad was now caught up in the rivalry between North and South, slaveholding and free states, and everyone realized that the railroad would bring crucial advantages to the side that built it. The road would boost manufacturing, settlement, and trade in the regions it served. In case of war, it would allow armies and supplies to move quickly from one

STUMPING FOR THE PLATTE VALLEY ROUTE

By the time of the Railroad Act of 1862, it had not yet been decided where the best route for the transcontinental line lay. But to professional engineers like General Grenville Dodge, who would take over as chief construction engineer for the Union Pacific, the "Mormon Route" via the Platte River valley and past the Great Salt Lake was the obvious choice. James E. Vance's *The North American Railroad* quotes the following explanation General Dodge offered in 1906, almost fifty years after the event, to an audience in Omaha:

There was no question, from an engineering point of view, where the line crossing Iowa and going west from this river, should cross the Missouri River. . . . The Lord had so constructed the country that any engineer who failed to take advantage of the great open road from here west to Salt Lake would not have been fit to belong to the profession; 600 miles of it up a single valley without a grade to exceed fifteen feet; the natural pass over the Rocky Mountains, the lowest in all the range, and the divide of the continent, instead of being a mountain summit, has a basin 500 feet below the general level.

General Grenville Dodge was the chief construction engineer for the Union Pacific Railroad.

western battlefield to the next. It would also tie the state of California to the region where it began, whether North or South.

As it became clear that the nation was headed for civil war, the northerners who controlled Congress were determined that the transcontinental railroad would follow a northern route. Historian James E. Vance explains:

> In 1861, when the southern states seceded from the Union . . . there was overnight a change in the political conflict, even in the face of actual armed conflict. Congress had an enhanced interest in advancing the cause of a Pacific railroad, to counteract the efforts of the Confederacy to detach the territories and western states from the Union.[4]

The transcontinental railroad would be built, and there was at least one man who had already done considerable planning for it.

THE SURVEYS OF THEODORE JUDAH

After finishing work on the Sacramento Valley Railroad, Theodore Judah considered the problems of his own transcontinental route. From past experience, he knew that locomotives could not haul trains up a grade much steeper than 110 feet to the mile. To cross California, however, his line would have to rise from Sacramento, at 50 feet above sea level, and cross the steep Sierra Nevada, where the lowest passes lay more than a mile higher. It must then descend to the dry plains of Nevada, at about 4,000 feet. As the crow flies, the total distance for accomplishing these elevation changes was slightly less than 200 miles.

Judah would not be put off by skeptics or discouraged by hardships. For him, the transcontinental railroad had become an article of faith. As historian Robert West Howard described Judah,

> He was, by birth and conviction, a Northerner and a devout Episcopalian. He perceived the utter impossibility of human "equality." Heredity and environment both denied that, and would keep on denying it. But freedom and equal rights to improve both individual and community environment were human birthrights. A Pacific railroad, as a technologic instrument that bound the Union

to its Pacific states and territories, was a vital step toward the achievement of freedom and equality of opportunity. The railway, then, was a project in ethical goals as well as military expediency and the economic realization of the Northwest Passage. As such, it must run through the freemen's territory of the North, rather than through the lands of the slavers.[5]

Doc Strong, a merchant in the Sierra mining town of Dutch Flat, California, had once told Judah about a possible route that followed the banks of the American River into the mountains. In the spring of 1860, Judah and Strong set out. They searched for easy grades and passes where the road could avoid expensive tunnels and bridges. The railroad must also avoid dense forests, as workers would have to cut a twenty-five-foot-wide swath of trees and remove their stumps—through digging or blasting—in order to provide a clearing for the roadbed.

Judah and Strong followed the north bank of the American River to Donner Pass. From the south end of Donner Lake, just east of the pass, they climbed down a steep ravine to the valley of the Truckee River into Nevada. Using his surveying instruments, and following a "sidehill line" that ran halfway up the slopes, Judah found that grades along this entire route did not exceed 105 feet to the mile.

In search of easy grades and passes through the Sierra Nevada, Theodore Judah and Doc Strong hiked past Donner Lake (pictured) and down to the valley of the Truckee River.

His next—perhaps more daunting—task was to convince potential investors that construction along this route would be feasible and a railroad across the Sierras profitable. Judah faced his share of skeptics, just as Asa Whitney and the other transcontinental dreamers had, before meeting a group of Sacramento businessmen. James McCague describes the scene:

> Judah unrolled his maps, spread out his sheets of figures and spoke, no doubt with his usual eloquence, outlining

his proposed route from Sacramento through Dutch Flat and on over the Sierras, dwelling on the benefits to be gained with the fervent conviction that always marked his statements about the Great Pacific Railroad.[6]

Judah conjured up a grand vision for the entrepreneurs of Sacramento. It was not his own vision of a heroic engineering feat, but a vision of fat profits from freight bills, paying passengers, and free land granted by the federal government. As historian Edwin L. Sabin described the situation,

> The fabulous Comstock vein had been uncovered, Virginia City had been baptized with a bottle of whiskey, the Washoe excitement had scarcely simmered down; the Nevada "Silverado" was eclipsing the California El Dorado, and the California stage lines, the Wells Fargo Express, and an army of freighters were doing a plethoric business between Placerville on the Sacramento Valley side and Virginia on the Nevada side. To shunt this business, or part of it, into Sacramento by rail promised a revenue . . . of $5,000,000 a year in the midst of its building program.[7]

Motivated by the money to be made following the discovery of silver in Nevada, Mark Hopkins (left), Collis P. Huntington (center), and Leland Stanford (right) helped found the Central Pacific Railroad Company.

Judah finally found his investors on Sacramento's K Street, at the hardware emporium owned by Mark Hopkins and Collis Huntington. Here he struck up friendships with Hopkins, Huntington, Chester Crocker, and Leland Stanford. These were practical men whose only goal was to make money, and the sooner the better. As they knew, the gold deposits of the Sierras had been played out, but a huge "mother lode" (principal source) of silver ore in Nevada offered even better chances for them as merchants, outfitters, and transporters. A railroad into Nevada promised a new opportunity for wealth. On June 28, 1861, the four partners founded the Central Pacific Railroad Company, with Leland Stanford as president and Theodore Judah as chief construction engineer.

Judah had estimated a cost of $12.5 million, or almost $90,000 per mile, for the company to build a railroad from Sacramento to the Nevada border. The partners of the Central Pacific were prosperous, but they could never raise that kind of money on their own. They needed help, in the form of land grants and loans, to pay for labor and materials. It was time to enlist the U.S. government in the cause of the transcontinental railroad. Fortunately, by this time, the government was ready to help.

THE GOVERNMENT ACTS

The Civil War had begun in April 1861, and for President Abraham Lincoln and the U.S. Congress the transcontinental railroad became a military and economic necessity. The railway would link California to the northern states as well as the Union cause. Having California on the Union side would deny Pacific seaports to the Confederate army and navy. It would also give the Union forces a strong western flank, if necessary.

By the time Stanford and his partners made their appeal for government help, Theodore Judah had been hard at work lobbying members of Congress for several years. A natural salesman and promoter, he had used every idea he could think of to gather interest and support for his project. As railroad historian Stewart Holbrook writes,

> Judah was a singularly well-posted mad man. Loaded to the brim with facts, as voluble on his pet subject as any congressman was on Patriotism or The Log Cabin, the

SKEPTICISM GREETS THE CENTRAL PACIFIC

Not everyone saw the transcontinental railroad as a noble and visionary achievement. Indeed, many Californians greeted the news of the Central Pacific with more than a little skepticism. According to Lucius Beebe and Charles Clegg in *Hear the Train Blow,*

> When Collis P. Huntington and his Sacramento partners in the hardware business started to build the Central Pacific in the foothills of the Sierra, their enemies in California politics called the venture "the Dutch Flat Swindle," intimating that it was planned as no more than a stub line to tap the traffic of the Mother Lode and connect with the wagon freight lines to the Comstock in Nevada. They declared the end of the line would be at Dixie Cut near Gold Run, and that only the gullible believed the "Big Four" intended to build across the High Sierra.

> The Dutch Flat Swindle remained a favorite theme for critics of the Central Pacific. In truth, the wagon road into the Sierras *would* bring the Central Pacific partners big profits—and the cash they desperately needed to carry on construction of the transcontinental railroad.

young engineer captured the imagination of both House and Senate, then went on to charm and hypnotize newspaper editors as well. Aided by Congressman John A. Logan, Judah was allowed to use a room in the Capitol and here he established what he was pleased to call The Pacific Railroad Museum. Here, too, he held forth from early morning until late hours, dispensing information about the road on which he said America's future greatness rested.[8]

In the fall of 1861, Congress began debate on a bill that would allow the U.S. government to finance a transcontinental railroad. Politicians spent months on the new law, balancing the need for the railroad against the questionable practice of making huge loans to private companies in a time of civil war. A Pacific Railroad Act was finally passed by the House on May 6,

1862, by the Senate on June 20, and signed by President Lincoln on July 1.

The bill granted the eastward-building Central Pacific and the westward-building Union Pacific a 400-foot-wide right of way along the final surveyed route. All timber, stone, and earth in the right of way became the property of the railroads, to be used for grading and construction. The grade could not be steeper than 116 feet to the mile. Curves could not be sharper than ten degrees.

Each mile the two companies completed would earn them a grant of sixty-four hundred acres of public land located within twenty miles of the completed road. For each mile, the government would also loan federal treasury bonds to the railroads, which would have the right to sell the bonds to the public. The bonds would not have to be repaid by the companies for thirty years; in the meantime, the government would make the interest payments to the investors.

The face value of the bonds depended on the difficulty of construction. For the easiest (flattest) sections, the government would issue $16,000 in bonds per mile. In the high desert plains between the Rocky Mountains and the Sierra Nevada, the amount rose to $32,000. For the toughest sections, in the mountains, the amount would be $48,000. In all, the government was loaning $50 million, interest-free, and granting twenty million acres of land to see that the transcontinental railroad was built.

The Congress directed the Union Pacific to build a railroad west from the Missouri River until making a connection with the Central Pacific. The law established no meeting point or boundary for either company. They were to build as far and as fast as possible. Their maps and surveys would have to be approved by the Department of the Interior, and their finished track would have to be approved by government inspectors. But in the end, every mile of track they laid would belong solely to them, to operate as they saw fit using their own locomotives and rolling stock. The Railroad Act of 1862 made the building of the transcontinental railroad into a one-on-one competition between two private companies, each generously financed by the U.S. government.

The law gave the transcontinental railroad companies exactly fourteen years, until July 1, 1876, to finish the job.

BREAKING GROUND

On the rainy morning of January 8, 1863, the Central Pacific partners held their official groundbreaking ceremony in Sacramento. While the citizens gathered on a muddy street, a band played from the front porch of the American Exchange Hotel. A banner reading "May the Bonds Be Eternal" hung across a flag-draped wagon, with the words appearing beneath the image of two hands clasping across the American continent.

Speeches were delivered by Charles Crocker, California governor Leland Stanford, and many other dignitaries. After workers brought two carts of covered, dry earth forward, the partners began shoveling the soil into a path marked between Theodore Judah's location stakes. The ceremony ended with

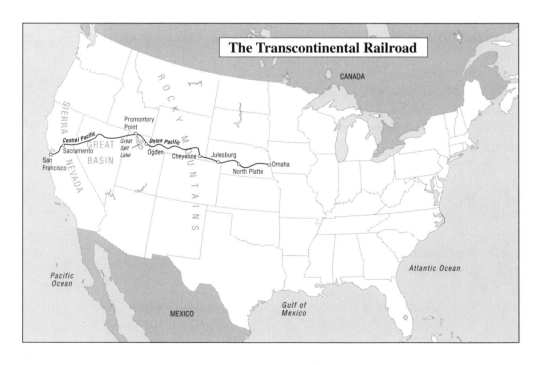

The Transcontinental Railroad

THEODORE JUDAH'S PROBLEM

Writer James Vance, in *The North American Railroad,* describes the problems faced and solutions found by Theodore Judah in his survey of the Sierra Nevada.

The Central Pacific had a hundred miles in which to climb seven thousand feet. If a perfect ramp for the distance were available, the climb would have been at a rate of seventy feet per mile, or 1.3 percent—stiff but manageable. Obviously a uniform ramp was not available . . . but with a steadily climbing line the locating engineers could hope to hold the ruling grade to around 2 percent.

Theodore Judah and his survey crew at work in the Sierra Nevada.

It was Theodore Judah who found that steady incline, not along the several routes where wagon roads had been cut through the forest and over the crest of the range, but along a new alignment that came to be known as the Dutch Flat Route, named for the mining camp where access was gained to the ridge that lay between the Bear River and South Fork of the Yuba River on the north and the American River on the south. Using the foothills approach to Dutch Flat, the critical ridge could be gained without any intervening valley to be crossed.

On both the Union Pacific and the Central Pacific the key [was] avoiding redundant grade—keeping out of any depressions that might lie across potential lines. In the Sierra the deep canyons meant that the grain of the drainage had to be observed and followed to avoid those declines that would make the line either excessively long or curving and to prevent unmanageable grades.

nine hearty cheers led by Charles Crocker. As the Sacramento *Union* reported,

> Everybody felt happy because after so many years of dreaming, scheming, talking, and toiling, they saw with their own eyes the actual commencement of a Pacific Railroad.[9]

Following a common early railroad practice, one of the partners—Crocker himself—had contracted to carry out the work. The contract made Crocker responsible for completing the railroad's first eighteen miles, from Sacramento to Roseville. To carry out the task, he hired several subcontractors who had responsibility for grading, tracklaying, and bridge building.

After the surveys were completed and marked, laborers proceeded with grading: digging and moving earth to build a level roadbed for the ties, track, and ballast (small stones laid between the ties for stability and drainage). While working along the north bank of the American River, the graders found only a shallow layer of topsoil. As a result, they had to dig far from the river and use horse-drawn carts and wheelbarrows to move enormous amounts of earth. The grading crews also had to reinforce the soft banks of the American River by placing large rocks and boulders, known as riprap, between the river and the Central Pacific roadbed.

In this early stage, moving earth and rock took longer and made the work more expensive than planned. Already, a shortage of labor was worrying the partners. Although Crocker and his subcontractors were paying workers four or five dollars a day—high wages for that time—labor was scarce and hard to keep. The partners and their superintendents scoured the mining camps of the Sierra and neighborhoods of San Francisco, Sacramento, Stockton, and other towns searching for willing laborers. For many Californians, however, the Central Pacific offered nothing better than a free pass to opportunities elsewhere. According to James McCague:

> Hundreds of workers hired out on the Central Pacific solely for the free transportation to railhead, then either kept right on going without ever touching shovel or pick handle or worked only long enough to earn stage fare over the Sierras to Nevada. The contractors took to bid-

THE IRISH COME TO CALIFORNIA

As workers quit the Central Pacific in early 1864, and those who stayed on began demanding higher wages, the railroad's labor problems grew critical. But the resourceful Charles Crocker had an idea. As described by historian James McCague in *Moguls and Iron Men,*

> Charley Crocker, not a man to be bullied by his own help and take it lying down, hit on the idea of importing Irish immigrant laborers from New York and Boston, where the slums teemed with them and they were despised by most Americans, regarded as fit for only the most menial and degrading of jobs.
>
> They were a raw and unskilled lot, most of them, ignorant, illiterate, but rawboned, willing, and strong as dray horses. They took to the work of grading and track-laying with that curious affinity the Irishman has always had for railroading in America. But they were wild, undisciplined, hard-drinking fellows, too. They did not all stick, and before long even the rawest of the ones who did began to grow wise to the labor situation, and to the uses of the strike and the slowdown.

Irish and Chinese workers are pictured blasting a route through the mountains.

Crocker knew that when the railroad reached the mountains, even larger gangs would be needed for steep grading, bridge building, and blasting out the mountain tunnels. Realizing that he would have to find an entirely new source of cheap labor to bring the Central Pacific over the Sierra, Crocker would turn to the Chinese.

ding against each other for the few who were willing to stick, with the result that wages were soon soaring. Even so the pace of the work lagged, with strikes and threats of strikes all along the line.[10]

There was no experience necessary or demanded on the Central Pacific. Men and boys of all ages were accepted. In his book *The Big Four,* Oscar Lewis writes:

> In 1865 Robert Gifford, age twelve, walked the four miles from his home in Dutch Flat to Gold Run, ambitious to help build this railroad to the Atlantic Ocean. A heavy, florid man looked down on him from the great height of a horse's back and told him to report to one of the gang foremen and to say that Mr. Crocker had sent him. Young Gifford remained on the payroll three months. His job was to lead a team of horses that pulled a dump-cart, and his wages were seventy-five cents a day and board.[11]

At one point, the Central Pacific partners even applied to the federal government for the labor of Confederate prisoners of war (the scheme ended along with the Civil War in April 1865). Another plan, to contract with Mexican landowners for the temporary use of peons (peasant farmers), also came to nothing. By some estimates, only two out of every five workers who signed up with the Central Pacific ever made it to the end of track to actually report for work. Most simply continued on to take their chances in Virginia City, the Nevada boom town where fortunes were being made in silver mining. Finally, the owners of the Central Pacific were forced to consider one last, desperate alternative: hiring California's Chinese immigrants.

THE QUESTION OF GAUGE

The labor shortage overshadowed another dilemma facing the Central Pacific: the fact that the gauge, or width of the completed track, had not yet been decided. Everyone concerned knew that the choice of gauge would be one of the most important decisions made in the construction of the transcontinental railroad. The decision was so crucial to the future of the road, and to the future rail network of the United States, that the Railroad Act of 1862 left the final decision of gauge up to President Lincoln himself. Lincoln, it was believed, stood above the greed for money and votes that motivated investors and congressmen. Members of Congress hoped that he would hear opinions from all sides, and then make a wise, unbiased decision.

Two standard gauges were in competition. A gauge of five feet would best suit the Central Pacific. In California, five feet was the standard used by the Sacramento Valley and other short-line roads. If Lincoln chose a five-foot gauge, Central Pacific cars and locomotives could pass easily from one line to the next. Local lines could be used as feeder lines for the main line to Nevada and the east, avoiding the expensive work of changing the fittings on locomotives and rolling stock.

Most railroads in the South also used a gauge of five feet. But railroads in the eastern United States used a gauge of four feet, eight and one-half inches. For eastern cities and businesses, this gauge would provide the least expensive link to the new markets opened by the transcontinental road.

On January 20, 1863, Collis Huntington of the Central Pacific called on Lincoln personally. Huntington brought Colonel George Davis, a railroad equipment dealer and expert on gauges, to persuade the president to adopt the five-foot gauge. Their presentation convinced Lincoln, who then called for a secret vote of the cabinet. The cabinet vote went Huntington's way, and on the next day, Lincoln signed an order for the transcontinental gauge to be five feet.

But the game was not yet over. Eastern politicians dominated the U.S. Congress. They represented business and railroad interests that wanted the smaller eastern gauge, which would hold *their* costs down. Bills were introduced in the Congress setting the gauge at four feet, eight and a half inches for the Central Pacific and its branches. The Senate and House both voted in favor. Instead of fighting the Congress on this issue, Lincoln decided to go along, and finally signed the measure setting the narrower gauge on March 3. This action set the gauge for the transcontinental railroad and for all future railroads in the United States.

THE FIRST BRIDGE

While decisions on the future of the transcontinental railroad were being made in Washington, the Central Pacific graders worked eastward from the outskirts of Sacramento. About one-half mile from the city, according to Theodore Judah's survey, the Central Pacific would cross the turbulent American River. This first bridge would have two main spans, each a 192-foot-long latticework of horizontal beams and vertical supports. Forests in Washington Territory supplied timber for bridge spans, while Pacific schooners brought massive redwood logs from northern California to be used for pilings (underground supports). To set these logs into place, workers moved a nineteen-hundred-pound steam-driven pile driver into the riverbed. With a steady, heavy pounding, audible for miles up and down the river, the hammer drove each piling thirty feet deep, down to the bedrock underneath the riverbed.

In the meantime, Theodore Judah ordered rolling stock and supplies from eastern factories. According to the Railroad Act of 1862, all supplies had to be manufactured in the United States. Shortages of materials due to the Civil War, and the high cost of freighting from eastern ports, made obeying this particular law expensive and impractical. Nevertheless, the Central Pacific's first locomotive, the *Governor Stanford,* arrived in Sacramento from the Philadelphia factory of Norris and Company on October 5, 1863. Five other locomotives, six passenger cars, as well as freight cars and coaches, had traveled in pieces by ship around Cape Horn to San Francisco, then were transferred to river steamers for the trip to the Sacramento yards.

After delivery, the locomotives and cars were assembled from the frames, wheels, and timber. Carpenters first made the simple flatcars, which were needed for carrying ties and rails to the "end of track." They later built passenger cars by nailing plank seats atop the car platforms.

On October 26, the Central Pacific laid its first rail. By November 10, the wrought-iron tracks reached the outskirts of Sacramento. To celebrate the slow but steady progress, the *Gov-*

According to the Railroad Act of 1862, all of the rolling stock ordered for the transcontinental railroad such as locomotives (left), flatcars, and supply cars (right) had to be manufactured in the United States.

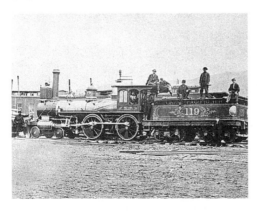
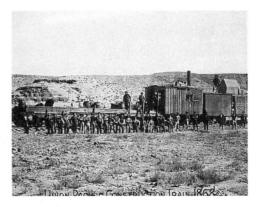

ernor Stanford was sent out on its maiden run. Crowded with cheering residents and distinguished guests, the locomotive steamed slowly forward along the two miles of completed track.

At Roseville, eighteen miles from Sacramento, the railroad made its first junction (with the California Central Railroad). At Newcastle Gap, thirty-one miles from Sacramento, workers built a station and depot. East of Newcastle Gap, the grade grew steep, and Judah's surveying stakes aimed the road directly through the middle of a hard, densely packed gravel mound eight hundred feet long and sixty-three feet high. Picks were useless; the workers had to set powerful gunpowder charges on top of the mound and then detonate them. Over several noisy weeks, the blackpowder blasting cut a narrow, dust-choked passage, just wide enough for a single train to pass, down to ground level.

THE WAGON ROAD

The Central Pacific had one other important construction project at hand: the Dutch Flat Wagon Road. This road linked the town of Dutch Flat, about fifty miles northeast of Sacramento, to Virginia City, Nevada, by following Judah's surveyed rail route through Donner Pass and into the Truckee Valley. Tolls from the road, the directors hoped, would help them pay their bills while waiting for track to be completed and trains to begin running. When the end of track finally reached Dutch Flat, the Central Pacific trains would feed even more paying passengers and freight to the wagon road.

The Dutch Flat Wagon Road proved useful as a source of cash, but it angered Theodore Judah, who saw work on it slowing down construction and drawing workers to the silver mines of Nevada, where they would be of no use whatsoever to the Central Pacific. Judah had several bitter confrontations with his directors, whom he suspected of trying to profit at the expense of the railroad. In a letter to his friend Doc Strong at Dutch Flat, Judah wrote,

> I had a blow-out about two weeks ago and freed my mind, so much so that I looked for instant decapitation. I called things by their right name and invited war, but counsels of peace prevailed and my head is still on. My hands are tied, however. We have no meetings of the board nowadays, except the regular monthly meeting

which, however, was not had this month, but there have been any quantity of private conferences to which I have not been invited.[12]

Judah was dealing with businessmen whose interest in turning a profit now clashed with his goal of building a lasting transcontinental route. For their part, the Central Pacific partners were growing impatient with their temperamental engineer. That fall, they finally offered Judah $100,000 for his interest in the railway, or control of the railway if *he* could buy them out for the identical sum. Judah accepted the challenge and prepared to meet with investors in the East. On board the *St. Louis*, just before leaving San Francisco harbor, he confidently wrote of his plans to Doc Strong:

> I have a feeling of relief in being away from the scenes of contention and strife which it has been my lot to experience for the past year, and to know that the responsibilities of events, so far as regards the Pacific Railroad, do not rest on my shoulders. If the parties who now manage hold the same opinion three months hence that they do now, there will be a radical change in the management of the Pacific Railroad, and it will pass into the hands of men of experience and capital. . . . If they treat me well they may expect a similar treatment at my hands. If not, I am able to play my hand.[13]

Judah felt sure that he, and not his four partners, would be credited with building the Pacific Railroad. But while traveling through the Isthmus of Panama, he contracted yellow fever. He died at the age of thirty-seven in New York on November 2, 1863, not knowing whether his dream would ever be realized.

MOVING MOUNTAINS

Judah had left for New York knowing that the Central Pacific desperately needed money. A short time after the railroad began construction, the company was several million dollars in debt. Materials were expensive; it cost more than $8,000 to deliver just one locomotive to California via the Isthmus of Panama during the Civil War. Iron, spikes, plates, and other materials had to be shipped from the East at exorbitant wartime prices and freight rates.

Workers wait near a paymaster's car for their wages. Because Californians in the 1860s did not accept U.S. government banknotes, the Central Pacific had to pay its laborers in gold coins.

Worse, the company had to pay its laborers in gold coins, as Californians of the 1860s did not yet accept banknotes issued by the U.S. government. This forced the Central Pacific partners to exchange the cash and stock they had on hand for gold—which sold at a premium over paper money. During one stretch of twelve days, the Central Pacific's bank account stood at zero—the company was unable to pay a cent for its bills or its workers. In order to attract investors, Huntington and the other partners had to pledge their own money to repay loans and guarantee stock investments.

But the railroad companies of the nineteenth century had many methods of staying in business. The Central Pacific helped itself by pulling off a neat geological trick: moving the Sierra Nevada westward. Judah had fixed the start of the mountains at Barmore, thirty-two miles east of Sacramento. In a case unrelated to the Central Pacific, the California Supreme Court had marked approximately the same boundary. The Central Pacific partners needed to prove Judah and the court wrong and that the mountains began much closer to Sacramento. The reward for doing so would be government bonds in the amount of

$48,000 per mile (rather than $16,000), the amount set by law for building in officially "mountainous" terrain.

According to the Railroad Act of 1862, President Lincoln would make the final decision marking the start of the Sierra Nevada. To convince the president of their view, the partners asked Aaron Sargent, a former California congressman and supporter of the Central Pacific, to meet with Lincoln early in 1864. Sargent brought with him a map showing that a change of soil—not elevation—marked the true geological boundary of the Sierra Nevada. He also showed the president letters from California's state geologist, Joseph D. Whitney, and from other scientists that supported his position.

Realizing that the financial health of the Central Pacific was key to completing the transcontinental railroad, President Lincoln decreed that Arcade Creek would be the western boundary of the Sierra Nevada.

Lincoln studied Sargent's material, perhaps realizing that he was being misled. Nevertheless, he too knew the railroad must get through—if not for the Central Pacific partners, at least for the sake of the Union. On January 12, 1864, he decreed that Arcade Creek, about eight miles out of Sacramento, marked the western boundary of the Sierra Nevada. For the twenty-four miles of level track running east from the creek to the Sierra foothills, the Central Pacific collected an extra $36,000 in bonds per mile that it could sell on the open market. The scheme gave the company a much-needed boost in its bank accounts in very lean times.

Lincoln's decision helped the Central Pacific to begin regular service on April 25, 1864. The earliest timetables of the Central Pacific showed three trains a day running the eighteen miles from Sacramento to Roseville. In the first week, the trains carried 298 paying passengers, bringing the line a net profit of $354.25. On June 6, the line was open to Newcastle Gap, twenty miles from Sacramento. Business continued to grow, and by the end of the year there were not enough passenger cars to handle the demand.

FALSE STARTS ON THE UNION PACIFIC

When the Central Pacific started regular passenger service at the western end of the transcontinental railroad, the Union Pacific Railroad and Telegraph Company still had little accomplished at the eastern end. The Union Pacific commissioners had first met in Chicago in September 1862, electing William B. Ogden as president and Peter Dey as chief construction engineer. For more than a year afterward, however, the Union Pacific would not lay a single mile of track or grade a yard of roadbed. It remained a paper corporation, without assets, income, or profits. It had only shares of stock to sell, and those shares stood for nothing more than the hope of a railroad operation halfway to California. The Union Pacific won attention and praise, but few stock speculators chose to risk their money in such a venture.

Dr. Thomas C. Durant led an energetic campaign to sell Union Pacific stock.

One man, Dr. Thomas C. Durant, a former medical student and railroad promoter from New York City, *was* eager to seize what he saw as a golden opportunity. Durant, elected by the commissioners as vice president and general manager of the railroad, turned out to be the individual responsible for much of the success, and many of the problems, of the Union Pacific Railroad. As described by Charles Edgar Ames,

> Dr. Durant was rather lean, somewhat stooped, with flashing, penetrating eyes and sharp features. His long brown hair, drooping dark moustache and somewhat

straggly goatee were worn in the style of the day. He dressed expensively and ornately, preferring to wear his slouch hat, finely fitted velvet sackcoat and vest, corduroy breeches, and top boots. In controversy, his manner was caustic and impatient; in salesmanship suave and persuasive.

Durant devoted his powers towards one goal. That was to make a fortune from contracts to build the Union Pacific, no matter how wastefully and regardless of where the chips might fall. . . . His basic theory was that the operation of any railroad would never, as a legitimate business enterprise, yield a profit, and the UP would be no exception.[14]

Soon after the Chicago meeting adjourned, Durant started a vigorous campaign to sell Union Pacific stock. He bought up shares on his own and persuaded others to buy shares by making the 10 percent "down payment" for the purchase himself. Durant made another very tempting offer: he promised to buy the shares in full if the purchaser ever wanted to sell. On these easy terms, he made sales to shipowners, bankers, railway operators, and to Tiffany and Company, a New York jewelry firm.

Although most people believed Durant was taking a very foolish risk, he did not see it that way. He had promoted the Michigan Southern, the first railroad to Chicago. He had helped to build the Chicago and Rock Island Railroad, and the Mississippi and Missouri. In all of these projects, he had managed to make money, even as the railroads themselves lost money or failed altogether. Thomas Durant knew there was more than one way to make money on a railroad.

SURVEYING THE PLATTE

While Durant peddled his Union Pacific stock in the East, in August 1863, the railroad sent out its first surveying parties. Their task was to find and mark the best route west from the Missouri River as far as the valley of the Great Salt Lake (the Union Pacific hoped to continue tracklaying as far as the California-Nevada line). For the first four hundred miles, the work proved easy. The surveyors hammered thousands of location stakes into the flat, grass-covered plains as far as the forks of the Platte

THE RAILROAD ACT OF 1864

In 1864, with the Union Pacific and the Central Pacific struggling, Thomas Durant, Collis Huntington, and other transcontinental railroad executives went to work on the senators and representatives in Washington, D.C. Sidney Dillon and Cornelius Bushnell, directors of the Union Pacific, lobbied President Lincoln himself and found the president willing to help. Bushnell recalled Lincoln's advice in Charles Ames's book, *Pioneering the Union Pacific.*

> Mr. Lincoln said to us that his experience in the West after many years was that every railroad that had been undertaken there had broken down before it was half completed. . . . He had but one advice to give us, and that was to ask sufficient aid of Congress, so that when we commenced the undertaking of building that road we should be able to carry it through to completion, and not break down and lose all we put into it. He said further that if they would hurry it up so that when he retired from the Presidency he could take a trip over it, it would be the proudest thing of his life that he had signed the bill in aid of its construction.

Congress passed the Railroad Act of 1864 in June; President Lincoln signed the bill on July 2. The act doubled the federal land grants, to 12,800 acres per mile, and gave the Central Pacific four years to reach the California-Nevada border. The act also allowed both companies to sell their own bonds, in addition to the government bonds, and in the same amounts that were due from the government for the completion of each mile.

Although the Railroad Act of 1862 gave birth to the transcontinental railroad, the Railroad Act of 1864, with its even more generous financial support, allowed it to be completed. Sadly, Lincoln's wish to enjoy a journey over the completed road would never be fulfilled.

River (at what is now North Platte, Nebraska). Between the forks of the Platte and the Salt Lake, however, the survey grew tougher. The crews had to cross four hundred miles of high desert and mountains, much of it still unexplored by whites and still an important hunting range for Native American tribes such as the Cheyenne, Sioux, and Crow. A route that would keep the grade under 116 feet to the mile was still to be found. The surveyors also had to determine the easiest crossing of the Continental Divide, the point in the Rocky Mountains that separated east-flowing and west-flowing rivers. Exactly where that crossing might be, nobody yet knew.

Complicating matters was the fact that the eastern terminus of the railroad still had not been decided. Several cities, including Omaha and Kansas City, were competing for the honor. According to the Railroad Act, the final decision of the terminus site would be up to President Lincoln (who owned land in Council Bluffs, across the Missouri River from Omaha). A bonanza in trade and a land boom would be the reward for the chosen city. By the fall of 1863, with the railroad ready to commence, a final decision was necessary.

In November, Durant went to Washington and arranged an audience with the president to discuss the matter. Secretary of the Interior John P. Usher was present at the meeting. According to Mr. Usher,

> Dr. Durant said, "Now the natural place for this terminal point is at the mouth of the Platte River. But Omaha is the principal town in Nebraska. The wealth of the Territory is there, and the energies of the people radiate from there. I think they ought to be considered, and the best thing is to start it from Omaha."

> I remember very well, Mr. Lincoln looked at the map and said, "I have got a quarter-section of land right across there, and if I fix it there, they will say that I have done it to benefit my land. But," he said, "I will fix it there anyhow." So that was the way it was done.[15]

On November 17, Lincoln issued an executive order, fixing the eastern terminus of the transcontinental railroad on the western boundary of Iowa, across the Missouri River from the city of Omaha. In other words, the transcontinental railroad would officially and legally begin in Council Bluffs, Iowa.

Unlike Lincoln's order on the transcontinental gauge, this decision would stand—but it would not be obeyed. The directors of the Union Pacific had to build their road as quickly as possible. The sooner they could finish track, and have it approved by government inspectors, the sooner the government would release bonds that they could sell to the public. Starting the Union Pacific in Council Bluffs, Iowa, meant that the railroad's first project would be a long, expensive bridge across the Missouri River. So Thomas Durant simply ordered grading to start in Omaha, on the river's western bank.

Here the Union Pacific's official groundbreaking ceremony took place on December 2, 1863. As Alvin Saunders, governor of the territory of Nebraska, turned a shovel of earth, citizens, mayors, and railroad officials looked on. George Francis Train, Durant's business partner, delivered a stirring dedication speech,

> The great Pacific railway is commenced at the entrance of a garden 700 miles in length and twenty broad. The Pacific railroad is the nation and the nation is the Pacific railway. This is the grandest enterprise under God![16]

Telegraph messages were read from cabinet secretaries, from Brigham Young, from President Lincoln, and from Leland Stanford, who sent a challenge as well as a greeting from the West Coast:

> California acknowledges with joy the greeting of her sister, Nebraska, and will prove her fraternal regard by her efforts to excel her sister in the rapidity with which, carrying the iron bands of Union, she seeks a sisterly embrace. Mountain and desert shall soon be overcome.[17]

The groundbreaking ceremony of December 2, 1863, however, proved to be the commencement of very little. The Union Pacific had recruited only a small company of workers and now found that most of the time it could not pay them. For equipment, it had only a few boxes of shovels and explosives that had been shipped to the Missouri River waterfront of Omaha. Through the winter of 1863–1864, the Union Pacific went nowhere.

THE OXBOW ROUTE

By March 1864, construction of a roadbed was finally under way in Omaha under the management of chief engineer Peter Dey and superintendent of construction Webster Snyder. The first graders were accompanied by fifteen women of the Omaha tribe, who each collected fifty cents a day for their labor. Workers

In March of 1864, work finally began on the Union Pacific portion of the transcontinental railroad.

began raising a sawmill, a machine shop, and a roundhouse on land laid out for a vast rail yard in the northern half of the city. A seventy-ton stationary "shop locomotive" arrived by oxcart after a long, hard journey across Iowa. On July 8, a Missouri River barge delivered the Union Pacific's first regular locomotive, dubbed the *General Sherman.*

On July 10, in Omaha, tracklayers dropped the first rail onto the grade, fitted it into "fishplate" connecting plates, and spiked it into the cross ties. About fifty miles of the route had been graded into a roadbed fourteen feet wide, lying two to three feet above the surrounding land. To handle storm runoff, graders prepared drainage ditches several feet deep on either side of the roadbed.

Meanwhile, the surveying crews continued their work, having split into three parties. One crew sought the best route from the 100th meridian in central Nebraska to the Black Hills of Wyoming; the second was to search for a suitable crossing of the Black Hills, and the third was to find a route between the Black Hills and Salt Lake. Peter Dey's task, in the meantime, was to complete the final survey of the Union Pacific line running due west from Omaha. As required by law, Dey submitted the plans to the federal government, and on November 4, President Lincoln approved them. After running due west for twenty-one miles, the line as Dey had marked it met the Platte River at the mouth of its tributary, the Elkhorn River.

Then, in December 1864, Thomas Durant suddenly called off the grading work. For reasons he did not explain to Dey or anyone else, he sent Colonel Silas Seymour, a personal acquaintance from Des Moines, Iowa, to "improve" on the route Dey had prepared.

Seymour came up with a new route that turned sharply south from Omaha, then west and northwest along the Papillon River. Seymour's survey added nine miles to the Union Pacific route, but its grades were not as steep. An easier grade was not the point, however. As Durant, Dey, and Seymour all knew, the added mileage would bring the company $144,000 more in government bonds, $144,000 more in company bonds, and 115,200 more acres of free land. These figures represented a tidy profit over the cost of completing the extra grading and tracklaying.

In addition to padding the length of the railroad, Durant was working to maneuver as much money as he could out of the Union Pacific itself and into his own pocket. With several partners, he set up a dummy corporation, called the Credit Mobilier, to handle the lucrative construction and supply contracts for the railroad. The Credit Mobilier was much more than a railroad construction business; as described by historian Samuel Eliot Morison,

> This was a company organized by promoters of the Union Pacific in order to divert the profits of railway construction to themselves. Fearing lest Congress intervene, the directors placed large blocks of stock "where they would do the most good"; that is, in the hands of congressmen. Vice President Schuyler Colfax and several Republican senators were also favored. These operations brought the Union Pacific to the verge of bankruptcy but paid the promoters over threefold their investment.[18]

Durant was determined that Seymour's "oxbow route" would go through, but his scheme angered Peter Dey. Writing to Grenville Dodge, a railroad engineer and Civil War hero, Dey offered his opinion of his employer:

SURVEYING IN THE MORMON COUNTRY

While Union Pacific surveying parties explored the plains and hills of Wyoming and western Nebraska in 1864, a party of seventeen under Samuel Reed rode through the Wasatch Mountains of northern Utah to survey the route as far as Salt Lake City.

In the 1850s, Brigham Young had brought the Mormon pioneers to this distant valley, where they had built the largest and most prosperous community between the Missouri River and the Pacific coast. A shrewd business leader, Young knew the transcontinental railroad would bring important changes to his community, and he intended to take every advantage he could from the new road. On his instructions, Reed's party of surveyors, guards, wagon drivers, and a cook were given a hearty welcome and allowed to purchase all the provisions they needed from Mormon farmers and merchants.

Brigham Young wanted the railroad to pass through Mormon territory.

Young's hospitality presented Reed with a serious dilemma, however. Reed had to decide whether to run the Union Pacific line through the Mormon capital of Salt Lake, on the lake's eastern shore, or to bypass the city and direct the Union Pacific through the smaller city of Ogden along the north shore. Reed knew that bypassing Salt Lake City would earn Young's anger—yet the Ogden route might prove shorter, easier, and less expensive. The Union Pacific directors would have to submit their final survey to the government before starting construction. If Reed decided on a route through Ogden, would Brigham Young fight the construction of the Union Pacific?

[The] Doctor needs common sense more than anything else, and I have been so completely disgusted with his various wild ideas that I have been disposed repeatedly to abandon the whole thing. I hate to do it as there is a great future in this thing, if judiciously and prudently managed.[19]

Dey finally did resign in January 1865. In the spring, to head off any further criticism of the new route, Durant threatened to begin the line at Bellevue, nine miles south of Omaha. Fearing the loss of the railroad, the people of Omaha immediately raised an uproar. The controversy, Durant knew, would pressure the federal government to accept the oxbow route, which, in turn, would "force" Durant and the Union Pacific to give up their plans for Bellevue and return to Omaha. That, of course, had been his intention all along.

Finally, in September 1865, President Andrew Johnson accepted the oxbow route that Colonel Seymour had surveyed. The president laid down one condition: The railroad must make needed cuts through the bluffs south of Omaha—which would take time and money—to ease the grade even further.

Durant ignored these conditions and ordered the grading crews to proceed over the Omaha bluffs. While the Central Pacific was making slow but steady progress up the western slopes of the Sierra Nevada, the Union Pacific had lost several months of fair construction weather to Thomas Durant's schemes. Better times, however, lay ahead.

BUILDING THE UNION PACIFIC

With the end of the Civil War, the Union Pacific had gained an important advantage over the Central Pacific—a ready supply of willing workers. Seeking good pay and adventure, thousands of men came out from the farms, factories, and battlefields east of the Mississippi River. Many of them were Irish immigrants, or the sons of immigrants, who saw little opportunity in the crowded slums of eastern cities such as New York, Boston, and Philadelphia.

Lured by promises of good pay and adventure, men came from the East to work for the Union Pacific.

Supplies now became the Union Pacific's most serious problem. Because Omaha still had no rail link to the East, most materials had to be ferried one hundred miles north from the Missouri River port of St. Joseph. Handcars, flatcars, passenger cars, baggage cars, and locomotives were also brought by steamboat along the Missouri. Other supplies arrived by oxcart after a 150-mile trip across Iowa from the railheads of the Chicago and Northwestern and Rock Island Railroads.

Materials, especially lumber, were still scarce. No hardwood forests grew on the Great Plains, and the only trees growing along the Platte River were spindly cottonwoods—unsatisfactory as a material for railroad construction. The wood was not firm enough to support wrought-iron rails or to hold the metal spikes in place. Over time, the spikes would come loose, the wrought-iron rails would wear down into the ties, and the rail surface would become uneven and dangerous.

Colonel Seymour devised a temporary solution to the cottonwood problem in the process of "burnetizing," named for the

The scarcity of materials such as wrought-iron rails and hardwood ties was a serious problem for the Union Pacific.

English chemist Sir William Burnett. The burnetizing machine consisted of a drum seventy-five feet long and five feet in diameter, in which 250 ties could be placed at a time. A steam-driven pump drew air from the drum, after which the ties were soaked in a solution of zinc chloride for three hours. Burnetizing made the wood metallic and heavier, helping to preserve it. Cottonwood remained a poor substitute for hardwood, however, and in later years the Union Pacific would have to raise and replace millions of the burnetized ties first laid between 1865 and 1869.

More durable wood was cut in scattered riverside forests north of Omaha and floated down the Missouri River on steamships. Omaha sawmills shaped the wood into lumber for boxcars and cut mountains of firewood logs for locomotive boilers. Burnetized cottonwood ties were used in the stretches between the rail joints, while hardwood ties were placed under the joints themselves, where stability was crucial. Three hardwood ties were also laid under the spur switches, where one set of tracks veered off from the main line.

GENERAL SHERMAN ARRIVES

Despite solving some problems, others remained. The Union Pacific still lacked money to pay its crews. Work progressed slowly— it took tracklayers eleven days just to get the first mile down. Then Thomas Durant wheedled a new investment out of Massachusetts congressman Oakes Ames and his brother Oliver Ames, who brought the Union Pacific desperately needed cash. By September 25, 1865, tracklaying crews had laid eleven miles of finished road. By October 28, twenty miles had been completed, and the Union Pacific was proceeding west at the rate of one-half mile a day. By the end of the year, the Union Pacific had completed its first forty miles of track and had begun limited freight service.

To celebrate the railroad's early progress, Thomas Durant organized a ceremonial joyride in November, inviting General William Sherman himself to take part. According to historian Dee Brown,

> To please Sherman they painted the general's name in gilt letters on Union Pacific Locomotive No. 1. As no passenger cars had yet been brought up the Missouri, they attached to the Iron Horse a platform car covered with

FINDING LONE TREE PASS

In September 1865, General Grenville Dodge was returning east after a campaign against Native Americans in the Powder River country, in what is now eastern Wyoming. While leading his command south through the Black Hills range, he made an important discovery. In his own words,

A rifle at his side, Grenville Dodge studies a map on Lone Tree Pass.

On September 22, after rounding up our stock, we continued our journey south. When we reached Lodgepole Creek, I took Leon Palladay and one of the other guides and about a dozen of the cavalry for the purpose of going up Cheyenne Pass to the summit of the Black Hills. I instructed the [wagon] train to follow along the trail at the base of the hills as far as Crow Creek.

We had proceeded along down the ridges keeping on the summit of the Black Hills for two or three hours, when one of the Indians with me discovered what he thought was a band of Crow Indians between us and the train. There was a large number of them, three or four hundred. I saw in a moment that we were likely to get into trouble. They had discovered us at about the same time. I watched them very closely to see their motions and saw that they were hostile.

upended nail kegs to which boards were fastened for seats. Sherman, Durant, Train, and the dozen or so men in the party wrapped themselves in buffalo robes and rode the fifteen miles to end of track at Sailing's Grove, where they picknicked on roast duck and champagne.[20]

Sherman remained unimpressed by the Union Pacific, and had his doubts whether the railroad would ever get through, saying, "I might live to see the day but can scarcely expect it at

I immediately dismounted my force and put the horses on the west side of the divide to protect them. We moved down in a body, holding to the summit. I knew with our rifles, which carried much further than any arms they had, we could keep them at bay. About 4 o'clock the cavalry discovered our smoke signals. I held to this ridge, followed it right down and saw that I was going down a ridge into the plains and I said to the guides and others with me that if we saved our scalps, I believed I had found a route over the Black Hills for the Union Pacific road.

I discovered that . . . I was on the divide between one of the branches of Crow Creek and another stream (Lone Tree Creek) and marked it very carefully by a lone tree. . . . When the engineers under my instructions came to examine it, they found a line with a grade not to exceed 90 feet. . . . Over this ridge which I came down, the Union Pacific railway was built.

Dodge's description appears in Charles Edgar Ames's *Pioneering the Union Pacific.* After his close call with the Crow, Dodge had discovered, by sheer luck, the easiest climb from the plains west of Cheyenne across the Black Hills. There, over Lone Tree Pass, the Union Pacific would build the transcontinental railway.

my age, when the two oceans will be connected by a complete Pacific railroad."[21] Sherman, like the Union Pacific's directors, knew that great sums of money were still needed, even though the Union Pacific's route appeared easy. He also realized that great obstacles still loomed ahead in the Plains—among them, the Sioux, the Crow, and the Cheyenne.

THE CONQUEST
OF THE
SIERRA NEVADA

While the Union Pacific sped across nearly five hundred miles of easy and level terrain, where in places not even a graded railroad bed was needed, the Central Pacific was preparing for the Sierra Nevada, which many people believed would never be crossed by

In many areas of the Sierra Nevada, passes through the mountains were a tight squeeze for locomotives and railcars.

a railroad. Before beginning the steep and dangerous climb into the mountains, Charles Crocker had hired James Strobridge as his construction superintendent. Strong and temperamental, Strobridge pushed his graders and tracklayers at a fast pace through the Sierra foothills. By June 1865, they had reached Clipper Gap, forty-three miles east of Sacramento. Theodore Judah's location stakes followed a twisting route along hillsides, over deep gulches, and through narrow valleys. From Clipper Gap, over the next fifty-eight miles to the summit of Donner Pass, the Central Pacific tracks would have to rise more than five thousand feet.

For Strobridge's laborers, the pay was steady but the workdays were long and hard. Many of them left the Central Pacific for mining camps; others staged strikes for better pay. Crocker and Strobridge realized that transporting more Irish workers from New York and points east was not the answer. The railroad needed money to ship materials, not workers, and would soon have to find an entirely new source of labor.

The last straw was a sudden strike at the town of Auburn, where several graders laid down their shovels and, in plain view of Crocker as well as Strobridge, demanded more money. Crocker turned to Strobridge, who was standing at his side, and instructed him to find and hire a gang of willing Chinese laborers. The strikers immediately and unconditionally agreed to continue working for their old daily wage.

CHINESE LABOR ON THE CENTRAL PACIFIC

Chinese immigrants had been arriving in California ever since the Gold Rush of 1849. After working and exhausting their own gold claims, many headed back to the port of San Francisco, where they found poorly paid work as servants, cooks, or gardeners. There was much anti-Asian resentment in California; Leland Stanford himself played on this sentiment to appeal to white voters during his political campaigns. As governor, Stanford had once promised to support any measure blocking Chinese immigration. Strobridge was even more adamantly opposed to hiring Chinese workers—but he would soon change his mind.

The bosses and workers felt certain that the Chinese would never be able to work as hard as European Americans. At first, Crocker hired the Chinese for the simple task of filling carts of earth for the grading crews. Later he put them to work driving carts as well as loading them.

When Chinese workers were allowed to begin excavating, Strobridge and Crocker realized they had been mistaken in their first impressions. The Chinese were tougher and stronger than they looked. They worked steadily and obediently, without complaints or demands. Having few prospects for employment elsewhere, they stayed on the job. Strobridge hired more.

At the work sites, the Chinese formed themselves into labor gangs, each with a head man who collected and distributed pay, took the orders from Crocker and the other bosses, and bought food from the group's earnings. The gang leaders spoke enough English to pass on instructions when the job could not be learned simply by observing.

From the start, the Chinese proved themselves capable of the hardest and most dangerous work the Central Pacific could give them. They stayed healthy by taking regular baths. They drank no alcohol and suffered no waterborne diseases, as they always boiled their drinking water. Their diet of rice, fish, pork, poultry, cabbage, noodles, and bamboo sprouts was brought forward on special supply trains from San Francisco. The Reverend A. W. Loomis, in the March 1869 issue of the *Overland Monthly*, commented that

> they are ready to begin work the moment they hear the signal, and labor steadily and honestly on till admonished that the working hours are ended. They have no story-telling; they have no sentinel set to watch while his companions enjoy their pipes, and to pass the word when the "boss" comes in sight. Not having acquired a taste for whiskey, they have few fights, and no "blue Mondays."[22]

By the end of 1865, seven thousand Chinese were at work on the Central Pacific. The railroad had solved its labor problem, but the presence of the Chinese still caused resentment in California. Workers in San Francisco and other cities accused the Chinese of unfairly competing with white workers and of causing a depression in wages. The resentment sometimes led to cruelty and violence at the hands of those who considered them rivals. James McCague explains,

> The despised Chinese was acceptable as cook, laundry-man, flunky, and handy butt for crude humor. But . . . working at white men's jobs? For white men's wages? By God, it was an insult, and no bonanza-chasing rowdy with a few tots of redeye whisky under his belt was going to stand for it! The fact that few indeed of these same stalwarts would themselves even consider swinging a pick on the railroad grades was altogether beside the point.
>
> In all the Nevada diggings it was considered great fun to make John China-man dance with the contents of a six-gun kicking up the dust around his frantic feet, or even to raid his encampments in the dead of night, set fire to tents and huts and send the heathen scurrying in highly comic panic.[23]

To ease the shortage of workers, the Central Pacific Railroad brought in Chinese laborers. They were not always welcomed by other Central Pacific workers.

CONTRACTING FOR THE CENTRAL PACIFIC

By March 1865, James Strobridge had realized the value of Chinese workers to the Central Pacific. To complete tracklaying over the Sierra, he needed more Chinese laborers—but could not find them. To meet the demand, he hired a San Francisco labor "contractor" named Koopmanschap, asking him to import as many as two thousand laborers directly from China.

Koopmanschap traveled to China and hired thousands of young Chinese farmers from the Canton region, where he recruited after the fall harvests were completed. The contractor advanced his recruits the fare for the ticket, which ranged from twenty-five dollars to forty dollars, depending on whether the laborers arrived by steamship or sailing vessel. (Steamship, the fastest and most expensive method, took a little longer than a month.) The money was repaid out of wages the laborer earned while in California.

Nevertheless, as the Central Pacific partners realized by the end of 1865, the Chinese were playing an important role in the construction of their railroad. Without their labor, the Central Pacific would certainly have a tough time overcoming its next obstacle: the summit of the Sierra Nevada.

INTO THE MOUNTAINS

In August 1865, the Central Pacific had reached the Gold Rush town of Illinoistown, where the line finally began pushing into the mountains. Here, the workers raised high embankments, fortified by heavy riprap and ballast, along the steep mountainsides. To build the embankments, they had to dig earth from the slopes and transport the loaded carts along broken, uneven dirt paths. There was little room to work; the pack animals had to be led carefully up and down the narrow trails.

The location stakes brought the line across long gaps, where the tracks crossed a river or creek valley. Trestles were needed across many of these gaps, as there was not enough soil available to raise earth bridges. The trestles were built on a frame of pine "legs" set in masonry and interlaced with horizontal beams. The tracks were then laid across the trestle tops.

Chinese laborers finish work on one of the many trestles needed to cross the narrow streams and steep gulches of the Sierra Nevada.

At the end of 1865, the Central Pacific reached as far as Colfax, 2,242 feet above sea level. The crews of tracklayers, spikers, and bolters lived in caves, tents, and shacks at the end of track; mule- and horse-drawn wagons brought supplies to the forward work sites from Colfax. Every day, two supply locomotives brought ties and rails that had been unloaded at the piers of Sacramento.

Along the way, workers built stations, water tanks, sidings, depot towns, and sawmills. To send reports along the route, the Overland Telegraph Company began operating a telegraph line alongside the completed track. There were now forests at hand to supply timber for ties, bridges, trestles, and for snowsheds that protected the track and trains from mountain avalanches.

After Colfax, the grade grew even steeper. The Central Pacific route climbed 3,400 feet in just twenty-eight miles. In several places, the road reached the maximum allowed grade of 116 feet to the mile. Central Pacific crews began excavating the first tunnels and soon became expert in the use of explosives. They blasted tunnels, cliff faces, and large tree stumps. A 100-foot-wide path had to be cleared of trees; every stump within the 25-foot-wide "embankment line," where the tracks would be laid, also had to be cleared. (If left in place, the stumps would eventually rot and undermine the roadbed.) Large trees that could fall across the track in a storm also had to be removed.

Shipping explosives to the work site presented another difficult and dangerous chore. An iron-walled, fireproof freight car carried the gunpowder from factories in Santa Cruz to the blasting sites. The car's doors were lined with rubber and its roof was made of tin. (In case of an explosion, a tin roof would give way quickly, directing the force of the blast up rather than to front, back, and sides, where it might derail the rest of the train.)

BLASTING AT CAPE HORN

In May 1866, the Central Pacific faced its toughest passage yet: Cape Horn. Here the railroad would run along the face of a cliff that rose a half mile above the American River. To carve out a narrow shelf for the grade, the Chinese workers were lowered in "bosun's chairs" (wooden planks suspended from ropes). Dangling above the chasm, they drilled out the holes for the blasting charges, tamped the gunpowder into place, and then cut and set long fuses. They were quickly raised to the cliff top before the charges went off. As Theodore Sabin describes the work,

> A bed had been literally chiseled from the granite slope so sheer that the laborers . . . were suspended by ropes while they hacked, drilled, and blasted 2500 feet above the rushing American River. Steadily making height, the iron trail bored on past the storied mining camps of Gold Run, Red Doc, You Bet, and Little York, startling the echoes with raucous blasts of the panting iron-train, signalling civilization's advance.[24]

Ahead of the graders and tracklayers, meanwhile, the surveying parties prepared for the summit above Donner Lake. On both sides of the summit, workers had to blast and prepare fifteen tunnels and build eight trestles of redwood and spruce logs. The longest tunnel, known as the Summit Tunnel, began

THE TROUBLE WITH NITROGLYCERIN

Invented by the Italian chemist Ascanio Sobrero in 1846, nitroglycerin exploded with three times the force and twenty-five times the speed of the same amount of gunpowder. It proved to be the most effective blasting compound yet—when workers knew how to handle it. Unfortunately, the mixture was unstable and extremely dangerous in the hands of inexperienced construction laborers.

Although the Central Pacific used this "blasting oil" in the Sierras, a series of tragic incidents eventually turned the Central Pacific directors against it. In April 1866, an unmarked nitroglycerin shipment was left in a yard of the Western Union building in San Francisco. Two curious workers on their lunch hour had poked through the crates, dropped one of them, and set off a tremendous explosion that blew them into pieces and killed several other bystanders. In the same month, at Aspinwall in Panama, a nitroglycerin explosion aboard the steamer *European* destroyed the ship and killed fifty people.

Blasting tunnels with nitroglycerine was the most dangerous part of building the railroad.

After these accidents caused a public outcry, and after several Central Pacific workers were killed in accidental nitro explosions, Charles Crocker decided to return to the reliable, and relatively safe, black gunpowder for the excavation of the Sierra tunnels. (In the meantime, a Swedish chemist named Alfred Nobel was devising a way to turn nitroglycerine into a safer paste form. Nobel's "dynamite" came just a little too late for use on the transcontinental railroad.) After a few months of hazardous use, and a public outcry, the Central Pacific permanently retired its entire supply of nitroglycerin.

twelve miles east of Cisco at the Central Pacific's highest elevation. The tunnel would be 1,659 feet long, 26 feet wide, 29 feet high, and run as deep as 124 feet beneath the surface of the mountain.

Work began on the Summit Tunnel in October 1865. The tunnel crews used wheeled carts to haul their tools and gunpowder up a steep mountainside to the tunnel face. Hundreds of charges were placed on either end, as well as on the top (once the track level was reached, workers could dig out from the middle toward the two ends, or "headings"). Blasting from the top progressed at the rate of seven inches a day. At the headings, the charges moved the tunnel inward at about nine inches to two feet a day.

When the blasting crews were busiest, the Central Pacific was using up to four hundred kegs of powder a day. When the tunnel crews began running out of blasting powder, Charles Crocker decided to try nitroglycerin, or "blasting oil," an unstable and dangerous compound of nitric acid, sulfuric acid, and glycerin. While separated, the ingredients were safe; ordinary Central Pacific freight wagons brought them up the trails to the workshop of chemist James Howden near Donner Lake. After Howden mixed the nitro, workers carefully moved small vials of the compound down to the work site to insert into the drill holes. Workers selected for their steady hands were employed in tamping the charges into the holes and then setting the fuses.

The Central Pacific used nitroglycerin to blast tunnels number 6 and 8 on the west slopes of the Sierra. The nitro was much more powerful than gunpowder, but it had disadvantages. On many occasions, the fuses failed to set off the charges. When that happened, the nitroglycerin was left in place. If an unlucky worker happened to hit the charge with a pick or other stray tool, chances of a sudden and fatal explosion were fair to good. In one such incident, supervisor Jim Strobridge himself lost an eye.

HEAVY WEATHER

The Central Pacific faced an entirely new obstacle during the winter of 1865–1866: one of the worst winters in local memory. Heavy rain and snow fell in the mountains, making the supply roads impassable for carts and wagons. Loose rocks and mudslides swept across the Central Pacific grade, damaging freshly dug roadbed. Search crews had to dig through deep snowbanks to find Judah's location line. At Gold Run, a stagecoach stuck in the mud had to be abandoned for six weeks. Instead of regular supply trains, the Central Pacific used mules and horses to carry food and tools to the construction camps.

The worst blizzard of the entire winter began on February 18, 1866. The snow fell for five days, drifting in some places to fifty feet deep. Supplies had to be brought forward by ox teams hauling sledges. When the slow-footed oxen bogged down, mules were used. If the mules could not get through, work stopped.

In the spring of 1866, the warming weather caused terrifying snowslides. One of the slides carried away an entire trestle near Cisco. At the entrance to tunnel number 9 at Donner Peak, twenty Chinese workers were killed in a single avalanche (their bodies were not found until the summer thaw). To continue laying track, deep trenches had to be dug in the snow, forcing the laborers to work in narrow, dark, and crowded passages among the snow and ice.

When the drifting snow finally made work on the line impossible, and supply wagons could not get through, Crocker sent crews ahead to blast tunnels, which at least were sheltered from the snow and the weather. Number 6 tunnel, at the summit, proved the hardest. The amount of rock brought up out of the tunnel was proving too great for the mule carts to handle. To mechanize the process, a locomotive from the Sacramento Valley Railroad was stripped of its wheels and sent ahead by oxcart over the narrow trails. The troublesome machine, nicknamed the Black Goose, proved just as terrifying to the pack animals as it was cumbersome for the men hauling it. According to James McCague,

Workers struggle to remove snow dropped on the Central Pacific tracks during the blizzard of February 1866.

A half-mile east of Dutch Flat the Black Goose began to assert her peculiarly baleful individuality. The occasion was a head-on meeting with a ten-mule rig coming downgrade. The mules took one look at the strange monster, snorted, laid their ears back and stampeded, leaving their wagon a wreck.

Not a horse or mule team encountered her without bolting out of hand. Finally wagonmaster Pratt hit on the idea of blindfolding every horse and mule that had to pass, and supplied Central Pacific teamsters to lead the hooded animals past the locomotive.[25]

Finally the Black Goose was set up on top of the number 6 tunnel shaft. The boiler was fired up and, with the use of a winch and conveyor belt, the machine began hauling debris up and out of the shaft. Even with the Black Goose in operation, the shaft progressed downward at the rate of only seven inches a day. Not until late in December 1866 was it deep enough for lateral digging and blasting to begin. Even then, work at both ends and in the middle progressed at a rate of twenty-seven inches on the best day.

DOWN THE TRUCKEE VALLEY

In the meantime, with deep snow stopping work at the summit, Charles Crocker decided to send supplies and graders ahead to Nevada. The partners knew that reports of winter trouble in the Sierras were frightening their investors, who were starting to believe that Theodore Judah's dream of building a railroad over the Sierra Nevada was indeed impossible. The partners urgently needed to prove that they could get over Donner Pass and continue laying track in Nevada. If they could not, Central Pacific stock would lose its value as investors sold out. With stock subscriptions drying up, the company would run out of cash; if unable to complete track, it would see the government stop issuing bonds. The Central Pacific would fail.

Crocker ordered three locomotives, forty boxcars, rails, fasteners, ties, and supplies placed on large sleighs and hauled by mules and workmen inch by inch along the narrow trails over the summit. On the eastern slopes, the rolling stock and supplies passed over "corduroy" roads made of logs lashed together. Using this method, enough hardware was sent ahead to lay forty miles of track in the Truckee Valley.

Crocker and Huntington were taking a very big risk by sending their supplies and crews ahead while the Donner Pass line was still unfinished. This newly laid track would not be eligible for bonds, as it was not part of a "continuous line," as required by the railroad acts. If the line did not get through in the

SNOWSHEDS ON THE CENTRAL PACIFIC

By the summer of 1868, the supply lines of the Central Pacific were extending across one hundred miles of high mountain passes. Fifty-car trains and larger were needed to keep up with the construction gangs working in the plains of Nevada. The Central Pacific bosses feared another slowdown in supplies just when they expected to make up for the months and years lost in the mountains. Speed was essential, but if rails, ties, and hardware had to be carted over the Sierras by mules and horses through snowdrifts and avalanches, the delays would continue. Between Cisco and the Donner Pass, at the highest and steepest points of the line, something would have to be done.

Wooden snowsheds were constructed to protect the Central Pacific tracks from avalanches.

The Central Pacific directors put the Scottish engineer Arthur Brown on the problem. Brown designed a series of wooden snowsheds to be built directly over the Central Pacific tracks. Six different gangs of twenty-five hundred workers raised the snowsheds. Eighteen-foot-long timbers were set into the ground vertically and then covered with roofs of four-inch planks. When sawmills could not keep up with the demand for new lumber, Brown used unhewn logs. On sidehills, where nothing blocked a snowslide's path to the railroad tracks, retaining walls were erected on the uphill side of the sheds. According to Brown's plan, the snow would accumulate atop the walls and, as it gathered weight, eventually slide off the snowsheds and into the valley below.

That winter, the snowsheds kept the line clear, while the Central Pacific completed track in Nevada at a rate of about a mile each day. Eventually, the Central Pacific would raise thirty-seven miles of snowsheds, using sixty-five million board-feet of lumber, and keep them in service for many years.

end, all of the expense would have to be borne by the company from its very small treasury. Far from speeding completion of the transcontinental railroad, these forty miles might well have ended the enterprise altogether.

In June 1867, as the Central Pacific was again making progress at Donner Summit, another problem arose. The Chinese gangs working in this region staged a strike, demanding a better pay rate of forty dollars a month and a shorter workday: ten hours in the open and an eight-hour day in the tunnels. Crocker responded by stopping the special food shipments, forcing the Chinese to eat the same boiled beef and potatoes that served the whites, and threatening to charge strikers the cost of keeping herds of pack animals for as long as they stayed idle. The Chinese soon gave in and thereafter never gave Crocker any trouble.

BYPASSING BRIGHAM YOUNG

Including rails laid in the Truckee Valley, the Central Pacific finished forty-seven miles of track in 1867. With the Union Pacific making rapid progress across the plains, Crocker stepped up the pressure on his crews to lay track quickly across Nevada. Crocker promised his partners and investors that the Central Pacific would attain the rate of one new mile of track a day in 1868. The Central Pacific had already sent surveying crews past the Wasatch range of the Rocky Mountains and into Wyoming, challenging the Union Pacific for the right to build east of the Great Salt Lake.

There were six hundred miles between the Nevada-California border and the Salt Lake Valley, where everyone expected the two lines to meet. Each mile completed, inspected, and approved here would bring in $32,000 in government bonds and allow the companies to sell $32,000 of their own bonds. An even greater prize, however, would be ownership of a railroad through the country settled by Brigham Young's Mormon community. Passenger fares and freight shipments through Salt Lake City, Ogden, and the other Mormon towns were sure to bring substantial profits when the transcontinental railroad was completed.

The railroad survey crews from both companies had searched north and south of the lake for the best location line. After completing their written surveys, maps, and elevation charts, they both concluded that the rough terrain south of the lake made a route that way, which would pass through Salt Lake City, much more difficult. General Dodge wrote in his autobiography:

> The northern route was shorter by 76 miles, had less ascent and descent, less elevation to overcome, less curvature, and the total cost was $2.5 million less. There was more running water, more lumber, and better land for agriculture and grazing.[26]

Going through Salt Lake City would add expensive extra miles to the route at a time when it was essential to get it finished and begin operating. After completing their surveys, the

Union Pacific and Central Pacific filed completed maps with the government showing planned routes passing north of the lake. These routes would miss Salt Lake City—Brigham Young's city— and pass thirty miles away through the town of Ogden.

When Dodge told Brigham Young about the planned northern route, the Mormon leader flew into a rage. He denounced Grenville Dodge from the pulpit of his church and made strong protests to the federal government. Young then promised to provide construction crews as well as plentiful food and supplies to the Central Pacific, if it passed through his city, and make passage much more difficult for its rival.

Despite threats and protests from Brigham Young, work progressed on the northern route through Utah, bypassing Salt Lake City.

Despite these threats and protests, the Union Pacific and Central Pacific held fast to their surveys. (Once they had filed them in Washington, they were legally bound to follow the indicated route.) Young could do nothing and, in the end, accepted the fact that Salt Lake City would have to be satisfied with a branch-line terminus. The Mormon leader did not lose out entirely, however. A Young family firm contracted much of the grading work for the Union Pacific through the Mormon territory, and Young allowed another Mormon company to contract for work on the Central Pacific.

TO THE HUMBOLDT

Meanwhile, Central Pacific gangs continued work on the still-unconnected stretches of the railroad. In May 1868, the Central Pacific tracks reached Lake Crossing, just west of the Nevada-California border. Used as a rest station by westbound emigrants before crossing the Sierra Nevada, Lake Crossing also made a good stop for the transcontinental railroad. From here, a spur line could be built to Virginia City, the booming Nevada silver town ten miles to the south.

Central Pacific construction crews set up a depot station at Lake Crossing, where Crocker's staff decided on a new name for the town to honor General Jesse Reno, a former military comrade. On May 9, an agent for the Central Pacific held an auction of the federal land to be granted to the company. The agent sold two hundred lots to the eager bidders, who had slept in tents and on open ground for the chance to buy. Immediately after the auction, the construction of the first homes and storefronts of Reno, Nevada, began.

From Reno the railroad continued along the Truckee River, then turned northeast past the Humboldt Slough, the source of the Humboldt River. It would follow the Humboldt northeast to the town of Winnemucca. In June, the gap in the line across the eastern Sierra Nevada was closed, allowing the Central Pacific to move supplies forward by rail all the way from Sacramento. The railroad transported its entire labor force to the end of track, and the Central Pacific began making rapid eastward progress.

Nevada was level enough, but it posed a different set of problems. Here the terrain was sagebrush desert with no forage, little water, and sparse rainfall. The few water springs that existed near the surveyed route were brackish, almost undrinkable. Laborers, pack animals, and locomotive boilers all needed water, so work crews were sent away from the main line to dig in the mountains for springs. After finding them, they sent the water back to the work sites via pack trains and newly laid pipes. Nevertheless, the water was often contaminated with salt and minerals, making the workers sick.

Despite the heat and lack of water, progress was good. The terrain here was flat and the location line had few curves. The loose, sandy earth proved easy to move and grade, and by this time the crews had been toughened by several years of work and by the Sierra crossing. The Central Pacific moved briskly

BUILDING THE TRANSCONTINENTAL'S TELEGRAPH

By the Railroad Act of 1862, the Central Pacific as well as the Union Pacific had to build telegraph lines along their right of way. Supply trains carrying ties and ballast for tracklayers also carried telegraph poles cut from spruce trees in the Pacific Northwest or cedar forests in the Midwest. The trains dumped the poles off at the forward unloading point, where telegraph crews nailed crossarms to the tops of the poles, dug holes, and drew the poles upright using ropes. The men then unreeled telegraph wire from a cart, brought it up the pole, and attached it to glass insulators.

After work for the day was completed, the telegraph wire was connected to a transmitter in the supply train's forward car. For the Central Pacific, the telegraph served as a crucial information network. The telegraph operator requisitioned materials from the supply bases in the rear and sent back information on the length of track completed for the day. From their telegraph office in Sacramento, the Central Pacific bosses transmitted needed information and orders to the end of track.

Linemen raise the telegraph wire that was used to report progress, request supplies, and transmit orders.

ahead at the rate of a mile a day, and more, just as Crocker had promised. Hundreds of tons of rails were shipped to the end of track every day, while grading tools were sent forward for the Mormon gangs working near the Great Salt Lake. Having crossed the worst terrain along the entire transcontinental route, the workers of the Central Pacific were now making up for their years of slow, heavy labor in the mountains.

5

TROUBLE ON THE PLAINS

The Central Pacific work crews were picking up speed, and the race was on to complete as much track as possible before the joining of the two railroads. The directors of the Central Pacific and Union Pacific realized that assigning a single contractor the task of grading and tracklaying—rather than hiring several competing, smaller outfits—would improve their chances of winning the contest. The Central Pacific directors had settled on a man they knew they could rely on: their own partner, Charles Crocker, whose tracklaying and grading gangs completed most of the Central Pacific line across the Sierra Nevada and Nevada.

The Union Pacific, under the direction of Thomas Durant, signed its major contract with General John T. (Jack) Casement and his brother, Daniel Casement, experienced tracklayers whose parents had migrated from the Isle of Man in the British Isles. The tough and wiry Jack Casement had served with honor on the Union side in the Civil War, proving an able leader; his younger brother was a skilled organizer. According to the agreement, the Union Pacific would furnish the Casements with all materials and haul them forward to the end of track for unloading. The Casements would furnish the laborers, who would be housed and fed at their expense. Over the next three years, the Union Pacific would pay the Casements from $750 to $1,100 per mile for the 1,046 miles of track they laid.

The job demanded speed, efficiency, and military precision. The Casements organized one hundred teams, totaling about a thousand men. (They paid $2.50 a day to ordinary laborers, $3 a day to spikers, $3.50 to $4 a day to ironworkers.) Their rolling camp of four 85-foot boxcars (twice as long as ordinary railroad cars) followed the construction site as it moved westward. One of the cars held an office, kitchen, and dining room. A second held

As their headquarters, the Casement brothers used a four-car construction train, which had offices, kitchen and dining facilities, and bunk halls.

a long dining hall, and a third both a dining hall and a bunk hall. The last car held bunks only. The boxcars could sleep about one-fourth of the entire force; the rest had to camp in the open or on the roofs of the cars. Alongside the Casement train grazed a small herd of cattle—the camp's main food supply—as well as horses and mules.

The Casements ordered supply trains made up in Omaha. Each train carried a precise number of ties, spikes, fishplates, and rails, which were unloaded on arrival at the end of track and then brought forward on smaller "lorry cars." After being hauled forward to the work site by horse, the lorry car was stopped and its wheels were blocked. Crews grasped a rail, brought it forward, and laid it in place. Gaugers then carefully checked the rail for any unevenness caused by ties lying at different heights. If a curved rail was needed, a large gang of men stood on the rail to steady it as ironworkers hammered down both ends to bend it.

The lorry car was then brought forward over the newly laid rails. Behind it came a car laden with spikes, which were dropped down in their places and driven home with sledgehammers. When the crews were working at full speed, each rail took about thirty seconds to lay and spike, and the line moved forward at a walking pace. Once all of its rails were unloaded, the lorry car was lifted off the track and wheeled back to the supply car. The next car then came forward.

Using this process, the Casements managed to bring the faltering Union Pacific up to speed. But for the workers, accidents, injuries, disease, and raids by Native Americans made surviving this job a chancy proposition. Historian Glenn Chesney Quiett described the life of the Union Pacific crews:

> Altogether, it was a rough, dangerous, dirty, sweating, hard-working, hard-drinking, free-spending life that this army of track-layers lived as they pushed the steel rails across the plains. They worked long hours under a fiercely burning sun in summer and bitter cold in winter, for the climate ranged the extremes. . . . In the late afternoon "time" is called. . . . If the money from the last pay day is not all spent, the men will probably wander into the town, that moving "hell on wheels," for a night of bad whiskey, gaudy dance-hall belles, crooked card games, and a morning-after headache. Of the raw nightlife of these camp towns it was written, "They counted the day lost whose low descending sun, saw no man killed or other mischief done."[27]

HELL ON WHEELS

Every hundred miles or so, Union Pacific workers raised a forward depot for the storage of ties, track, and hardware. Each of these depots had switches, sidings, and a station for passengers and freight. New towns appeared around the depot as the work was completed. North Platte, Nebraska; Julesburg, Colorado; Cheyenne, Wyoming; and several other modern-day cities had their origins as Union Pacific depot towns.

Most railroad towns sprang up overnight and disappeared just as quickly as the line moved on. Entire buildings—hotels, dance halls, shanties—were moved along the railroad from one point to the next as the work progressed. The mobile town was no place for the faint of heart. Described by newspaper publisher Samuel Bowles as a "Hell on Wheels," it served a rough, roving population of drifters, confidence tricksters, gamblers, and prostitutes whose customers and victims consisted of Union Pacific work crews. Life for the inhabitants could be violent and short; Julesburg proved so dangerous to the health and welfare

THE FORSAKEN VILLAGE OF BEAR TOWN

In his book, *Pioneering the Union Pacific,* railroad historian Charles Edgar Ames describes the sad fate of Bear Town (also known as Bear River City), Wyoming—the scene of the bloodiest fight among white men in the entire bloody frontier history of Wyoming.

When the UP graders bore down on Bear Town in the autumn of 1868, the nefarious crowd from Green River also moved in, creating still another Hell-on-Wheels of nearly 2,000 persons, with well over a hundred shacks, log cabins, tents, and saloons. A character by the name of Leigh Freeman, editor of a local newspaper called The Frontier Index, assumed leadership of an aggressive group of merchant vigilantes, it seems, and started to clean up the town, not distinguishing much between the Green River riffraff and some hard drinking UP graders. A misfit, irresponsible Southerner, Freeman next printed outrageous personal attacks on newly elected President Grant, respected by all workers on the railroad.

Soon the inevitable riot came off. About November 19, a large group of Union veterans and Irishmen apparently broke open the jail, released their pals, and advanced on The Frontier Index hovel. They were said

of Union Pacific workers that General Grenville Dodge, whom Durant had hired as chief engineer, brought in Jack Casement himself to clean it up.

The former general approached the assignment in military fashion and went to work over the July 4 holiday of 1867. He handpicked a squad of good shots and ordered another squad to stand by in the vicinity just in case. The men marched into Julesburg and immediately shot down anybody that pulled a gun. They then marched several dozen others to a cottonwood grove for a quick hanging, and shipped all prostitutes known to be infected with venereal disease out of town. As Grenville Dodge describes it,

I wired him, "Go and clean the town out. Hold it until the citizens are willing to obey orders of the officers I place to be armed only with picks and shovels, and were easily mowed down on the street by vigilante rifle fire from cabins. At least 14 UP men were killed and dozens more wounded. Embroiling white men could hurt the UP more than the Indians could.

The track reached Bear Town only days later, but the trains passed by without a stop. Not so much as a siding was put in. Thus ruined, the vigilantes began to move away, and soon Bear River City became just a bad memory.

Railroad towns such as Bear Town were often plagued by bloody acts of violence.

in charge." This was fun for Casement. When I saw him later, he said, "I will show you what I did." He took me to a hill where there was quite a burial ground and he said, "General, they all died in their boots and Julesburg has been quiet since."[28]

Despite the law and order imposed by Casement in Julesburg, riotous camp followers remained a problem for the Union Pacific.

FIGHTING FOR THE LAND

Keeping order in the railroad towns and camps was hazardous enough. To make matters even more dangerous, Union Pacific workers had to fight an endless running battle with Native Americans all along the right of way. The Sioux, Cheyenne, and Crow attacked surveying parties, tracklaying gangs, and grading crews throughout Nebraska and in eastern Wyoming, where they saw ancient hunting grounds and their nomadic way of life threatened by the arrival of the "iron horse."

The war parties staged hit-and-run raids at all hours of the day, and sometimes at night, forcing the Union Pacific crews to

Because the railroad passed through Native American lands, work crews were often attacked by warriors defending their ancient hunting grounds.

post sentries and supply rifles to all hands. The Casement train carried an arsenal of weapons to the end-of-track work sites. To provide further protection, the U.S. Army built posts at Fort Kearney, Fort McPherson, and Fort Sedgwick along the Platte River, and at Fort Russell, Fort Laramie, and Fort Bridger in Wyoming. Under the command of General William Sherman, these posts had standing orders to provide protection and provisions to the work crews when necessary. But even with the assistance of the allied Pawnee, Sherman's small and scattered cavalry units could not cover the entire route or protect all the Union Pacific workers. According to Grenville Dodge:

> Our Indian troubles commenced in 1864 and lasted until the tracks joined at Promontory. We lost most of our men and stock while building from Fort Kearney to Bitter Creek. At that time every mile of road had to be surveyed, graded, tied, and bridged under military protection. The order to the workers was never to run when attacked. All were required to be armed.[29]

HITTING AND RUNNING

Hundreds of small battles took place during the construction of the eastern half of the transcontinental railroad. On May 18, 1867, a band of eight hundred Native Americans pulled up surveying stakes near Ogallala, Wyoming, while the surveying crew hid in the nearby hills. On May 25, five men were killed near Overton, Nebraska. On the same day, at the end of track, a band of Sioux killed three workers. Near Ogallala, on May 27, General Dodge himself and a party of three government commissioners came under attack while inspecting newly laid track. The braves cut several mules and horses from a gathered herd,

THE RAID AT PLUM CREEK

The most famous raid in Union Pacific history took place on August 6, 1867. Led by Chief Turkey Leg, a band of Cheyenne swept down on a section of completed track 4 miles west of Plum Creek and 230 miles east of Omaha. After scattering a few gathered workers, the braves cut down the adjoining telegraph wire and used it to fasten a tie to the surface of the rails. Then they waited for an oncoming train.

The break in the telegraph wire was soon detected. A lineman, William Thompson, brought a crew of five out on a handcar to inspect the break. Spotting the tie too late to avoid it, they leaped off the handcar just as it hit the tie and flipped over. The men scattered. A Cheyenne named Red Horse caught up with Thompson, shot him in the arm, and then scalped him. Red Horse grabbed the scalp but dropped it as he rode away. Still alive, Thompson played possum until making sure all was quiet, then retrieved his scalp. He began walking alone back to Willow Island station.

During the Plum Creek Raid, a second train arrived, but it was able to back away at full speed to safety.

Turkey Leg's band then tore up the rails and piled them across the tracks with more ties. A five-car freight train, hauled by locomotive No. 53, hit the obstacle at full speed. The engine derailed and immediately caught fire; engineer Brookes Bowers and fireman Gregory Henshaw were killed. The natives looted the boxcars of calico, tobacco, sugar, coffee, hats, ribbons, and whiskey, ate all the food they could hold, dressed themselves and their ponies in the stolen goods, and set the rest of the train on fire. Another train showed up in the middle of the raid, but its engineer stopped just before reaching the wreckage and then backed up full speed to Plum Creek.

General Dodge was called in the next day and drove the Cheyenne off. Despite a determined effort, however, William Thompson's doctors were unable to graft his scalp back onto his head. It was finally preserved in a jar of formaldehyde and donated to the Omaha Public Library, where it remained on display for many years.

while Dodge and the commissioners ran to a nearby railcar for rifles. Dodge managed to chase off the raiders without any casualties. After the commissioners made their report, the army stationed three more cavalry companies along the line.

The raids continued through the summer. On July 5, near the new depot town of Cheyenne, Sioux braves killed two men, who thereby became the town's first permanent inhabitants. On August 4, 1867, a band of Cheyenne attacked the completed Union Pacific tracks four miles west of Plum Creek, and 230 miles west of Omaha, where regular supply trains were running every day.

Although armed crews managed to stop most of the raids, Native American bands continued harrying Union Pacific locomotives. Often a group of mounted raiders would ride alongside the train, firing scattered rifle shots or arrows at the locomotive in an attempt to hit the crew. Other times, a barricade of torn-up ties and rails would be set across the tracks to derail the trains. Troublesome as these incidents were, the Union Pacific did not allow them to stop construction. The Union Pacific directors knew that the sooner the line could start running, and the more settlers could be brought to this country, the faster the U.S. government would seek to resolve the Native American uprisings by all-out war or by treaty.

ACROSS THE DIVIDE

By the beginning of 1868, the Union Pacific tracks had left Nebraska behind and reached Granite Canyon, on the eastern slope of the Black Hills of Wyoming. In the early spring, the construction gangs left their winter camp near Cheyenne. Nearly two thousand graders set out to prepare the roadbed over the Black Hills, while several hundred others cut timber in the surrounding forests for use as ties.

According to John Stover, the hasty work led to shoddy and dangerous construction:

> The construction was often hurried with flimsy bridges, narrow embankments, and improperly ballasted track. General Dodge himself admitted that his company's greedy insistence on continued construction in the winter months often doubled or even tripled building costs. The haste in construction was also caused by a public that wished to see the job completed.[30]

At 8,242 feet, Sherman Summit is the highest point along the transcontinental railroad.

But the steadily advancing tracklaying crews had finally convinced investors that there would be a completed transcontinental railroad. As federal inspectors approved forty-mile sections of the road through Nebraska and Wyoming, the government released its bonds for the company to sell. Because investors now had more confidence in the project, buyers could no longer purchase Union Pacific bonds at a large discount to their face value of $100. On May 21, 1868, Oliver Ames, the Massachusetts businessman and congressman who had invested a fortune in the Union Pacific, sold about $2 million worth of government and company bonds, for miles 540 through 580, at $99.50 each.

Freight hauling and passenger service on the completed portion of the line also brought money into the company's treasury. For example, the Union Pacific signed a contract with the U.S. Post Office to carry the mail between Omaha and Cheyenne at the rate of $150 per mile per year. The railroad also signed a contract with Thomas Wardell and C. O. Godfrey, who agreed to operate coal mines in the Union Pacific's right of way and to supply coal to the railroad at a discounted price.

Better protection gave the freighters confidence that their goods would get through safely. Using Fort Russell as headquarters, the U.S. Army had posted five thousand troops along the route from Nebraska to Salt Lake City to protect the trains and work crews.

On April 5, 1868, the Union Pacific tracks reached the Continental Divide at Sherman Summit, the highest point of the entire transcontinental line at 8,242 feet. Soon afterward, bridge gangs completed the 600-foot Dale Creek Bridge across a 120-foot gorge. The Casement train made rapid progress down the western slope of the Divide. On the route between Fort Steele and Granger—both in Wyoming Territory—tracklayers worked at the rate of 2.3 miles every day. On one record-setting day, the Casement brothers saw their crews put down 8.5 miles. On another, the tracklayers actually caught up with the grading crews and were forced to halt. The downtime still profited the Casement brothers, who, according to their contract with the Union Pacific, collected three thousand dollars for every day they had to wait for the graders to finish work ahead of the track.

The Union Pacific and Central Pacific were now engaged in a mad dash for the final meeting point. A great deal of money was at stake for shareholders and partners, and the competition led to daring games of financial one-upmanship. When Chester Crocker heard the news of eight miles laid by the Union Pacific tracklayers in a single day, he replied by promising that the Central Pacific would lay ten. When Thomas Durant heard Crocker's promise, he bet a cool ten thousand dollars that the Central Pacific could not do it.

Meanwhile, a lull in hostilities between the railroad and the Native Americans was brought about by the Fort Laramie treaty, which the United States signed with Chief Red Cloud's band of Sioux in July 1868. The treaty closed the Bozeman Trail, which gold prospectors were using in Montana Territory, and granted much of northeastern Wyoming to the Oglala Sioux. For the time being, eastern Montana would belong to the Native Americans for their spring and summer buffalo hunt.

The Fort Laramie treaty was honored only temporarily, however. Eventually, as William Withuhn writes, the railroad spelled doom for the way of life of Native Americans on the plains.

> In the early wars to defend their ancestral lands against white settlers, Indians could steal guns and outmaneuver the invaders. Against the railroad in the end, however, they could do nothing, for the railroads brought settlers in such huge numbers that resistance became futile.[31]

For the time being, the Union Pacific could lay its track in peace. After crossing the Black Hills at Sherman Summit, the railroad turned northwestward across the Laramie Plains. The tracks crossed the North Platte River and then the Red Desert be-

MAKING PEACE WITH THE PAIUTE

While Union Pacific workers were fighting Native Americans on the Plains, the Central Pacific enjoyed a crucial advantage in its relations with Native Americans. According to historian James McCague in *Moguls and Iron Men,*

> Charley Crocker had worked out a unique solution for his own problem. The Paiute chiefs were sought out and presented with passes good on all passenger trains. Trainmen were instructed to let the common braves and their squaws ride in the freights unmolested. In return a solemn pledge of no interference with the railroad or its workers was exacted from the Indians.
>
> Contrary to the usual fate of such treaties in the sorry history of Indian-white relations on the frontier, this one was honored on both sides. The system worked so well with the Paiutes that it was soon extended to the Shoshones, too. So Central Pacific supply trains and drag freights rolled out along the Truckee and on across Nevada with dignified aborigines squatting on the car tops, and peace prevailed.

fore reaching the basin of the west-flowing Bitter Creek River. Farther west lay the Green River, a tributary of the Colorado.

Here the Union Pacific reached the northern edge of the Uinta Mountains and the town of Aspen, Wyoming, at an elevation of 7,540 feet. The line followed the Bear River, then crossed into Utah territory and the Wasatch Mountains. Just beyond Echo, in Weber Canyon, Utah, the Union Pacific gangs laid their one-thousandth mile of track. The crews worked straight through the winter of 1868–1869, digging two tunnels through Weber Canyon and raising a trestle made from 180,000 board-feet of timber across the gorge. Echo Canyon and Weber Canyon would be the last difficult stretches before the line followed the Weber River down to the valley of the Great Salt Lake.

THE RAILROADS CROSS

While tracklayers hurried to get rails, ties, and ballast down in the plains, deserts, and mountain valleys, Union Pacific and Central Pacific surveying crews had been working well ahead of the grading crews. The rival surveyors met, then passed each other, both measuring the same land and marking their maps with similar routes. Historian Oliver Jensen describes conditions:

> An amendment to the Pacific Railroad Act had left the meeting place of the two companies indefinite. As a result . . . rival surveying and grading crews pushed past each other on parallel lines for hundreds of miles. As the grading crews began working close to each other, the Irish [workers for the Union Pacific] began rolling boulders down on Chinese crews [for the Central Pacific], or setting charges near them without warning, but the Chinese gave as good as they got.[32]

Central Pacific surveyors explored the hills of western Wyoming, while Union Pacific gangs were working in eastern Nevada, well to the west of the Great Salt Lake. Although General Dodge protested this work, which he saw as a waste of money, Durant ordered the surveys made and demanded that tracklaying crews push ahead.

Durant's orders led to an expensive miscalculation in the fall of 1868. For the sake of getting four, five, or more miles of track laid in a day, he ordered grading crews to move back and help with the ties and tracklaying. For several weeks, the grading was neglected as the weather grew colder and the ground grew harder. Then, in December 1868, when grading resumed in northern Utah, the workers had to use explosives to soften up the frozen earth before digging. This time-consuming step proved much more expensive than grading dry ground would have been earlier in the fall.

Under orders from Durant to lay four or more miles of track per day, grading crews help tracklayers reach the goal.

As the two railroads moved toward each other, the hazards and difficulties of the job lessened. There was plenty of cash on hand, labor was plentiful, and supplies less expensive. The Union Pacific had temporarily solved the problem of Native American raids; the Central Pacific had overcome the high Sierra. Sometime in early 1869, the transcontinental railroad would be completed as the two lines joined. But where?

MEETING AT PROMONTORY

By November 1868, Central Pacific crews had reached Palisade Canyon in eastern Nevada. Here the tracklayers worked in long, deep granite canyons, with walls so steep and high that sunlight rarely reached their floors. Following the Humboldt River, the crews worked their way through Carlin Canyon as the sharp winter winds howled south across the desert and heavy morning and evening fogs hampered work. Twenty miles farther east lay the town of Elko, Nevada, a silver-mining boomtown. The Central Pacific reached Elko on Christmas Day, then stopped for the year, having laid 363 miles of track across the Nevada deserts.

A train crosses the trestle at Echo Canyon, Utah.

Meanwhile, Central Pacific surveyors mapped out a route past Promontory, on the north side of Great Salt Lake, to Echo Canyon. The railroad submitted the survey to the government. Secretary of the Interior Orville Browning approved the survey—even while Union Pacific grading crews were at work in the same area. When the Union Pacific directors heard of this action, they lodged a strong protest with the secretary. Browning backed down, saying that he had only wanted to make sure the two tracks would meet somewhere. He also declared that both companies had the legal right to survey as much land as they wished.

MEETING WITH PRESIDENT GRANT

In the spring of 1869, the rival railroads were working toward each other in the rocky hills north of the Great Salt Lake.

It was March when Union Pacific tracklayers swung through Devil's Gate, the defile that tumbles Weber River out on the east slope of the Salt Lake Valley. They raised a last, long bridge across the Weber River. The bridge, Mormon elder John Taylor wrote to the *Deseret News,* "has in it, I am informed, 180,000 feet of timber and was put up in one week . . . the mountain sides have fallen, the valleys have been exalted, the pathway has been made through the mountain fastness and the railroad is now a *fait accompli.*"[33]

By the end of March the Union Pacific graders had reached Blue Creek, ten miles east of the tiny town of Promontory, Utah.

President Ulysses S. Grant was influential in determining where the Union Pacific and Central Pacific railroads would meet.

Meanwhile, Central Pacific crews were working by lamplight late into the night, over easier terrain, to make up for time lost in the Sierras.

The Union Pacific and Central Pacific had still not decided on a meeting point. In this region each mile of track laid was worth almost $100,000 to the two companies in the form of bonds and land. Samuel Montague and Grenville Dodge both realized that they were wasting money and effort by having their surveying crews work past each other. But their bosses—the rival directors and officers—could still not reach an agreement.

In late March, the newly inaugurated president, Ulysses S. Grant, summoned Grenville Dodge to Washington for an important meeting. Grant promised that if the two companies could not agree on a meeting point, he would have the government fix one. Another meeting was then arranged between Durant, Dodge, and Collis Huntington. After several days of bickering, the two companies finally managed to come to an agreement. On April 10, a resolution agreed to by the two companies was read into the congressional record by Senator Jacob Howard.

Resolved: that the common terminus of the Union Pacific and the Central Pacific Railroads shall be at or near Og-

WORKING AND SETTLING IN THE MORMON COUNTRY

At first angered by the bypassing of his capital at Salt Lake City, Brigham Young later came around as an enthusiastic supporter of the transcontinental railroad. Mormon firms had taken on much of the construction in the territory, with the Mormon firm of Benson, Farr, and West grading for the Central Pacific and Sharp and Young (owned by Brigham Young's son Joseph) working for the Union Pacific.

The arrangement helped both the Mormon community and the railroad. Always short of cash to pay his workers, Thomas Durant persuaded the Mormon firms to accept reduced rates for grading, tunneling, and masonry work. In exchange, Durant granted Mormon settlers lowered passenger fares for transportation to Utah from the east. This arrangement proved a great boon to the settlement of the Mormon territory for the rest of the nineteenth century.

den; and the Union Pacific Railroad Company shall build, and the Central Pacific Railroad Company shall pay for and own, the railroad from the terminus aforesaid to Promontory Point, at which point the rails shall meet and connect and form one continuous line.[34]

The Union Pacific made swift progress up the eastern slope of the Promontory Ridge. There was now little room left for Charles Crocker to fulfill his boastful promise of the year before. On April 27, Crocker announced that the Central Pacific, on the very next day, would lay ten miles of track.

BREAKING ALL RECORDS

Crocker and Strobridge selected 848 men for the task, as well as two four-man iron-laying crews. The crews broke camp at dawn and moved forward to the end of track. Their progress that day would take them over the Rozell Flats, which gradually ascended toward Promontory Summit. The Union Pacific declared a work holiday, and laborers as well as several Union Pacific bosses, including General Jack and Dan Casement, rushed forward to

J. H. Strobridge (center, with beard) stands at the Central Pacific camp at Victory, Utah. It was over this section that crews laid a record-breaking 10 miles of track in one day.

observe. Central Pacific president Leland Stanford had arrived from California; citizens from the nearby towns of Corinne and Blue Creek as well as officers and enlisted men of the U.S. Army came out for the event.

Just after dawn, at a signal from Crocker, the work began. As Robert West Howard describes it,

> The Chinese, trotting in quick step, literally danced the ties from wagons to roadbed on a bobbing belt of denim and coolie hats. The eight Irishmen paced behind them, heaving 120 feet of rail a minute from the car, racing it to the ties—and stepping smartly aside so the spikers and fishplate men could move in. All without one misstep.[35]

Six miles of track were laid by the time Strobridge called for the midday break at 1:30 in the afternoon. An hour later, work began again, finally halting at 7:00 P.M. at a completed distance of ten miles, two hundred feet of track. The workers had put down 25,800 ties, 55,000 spikes, 3,520 rails, and 7,040 fishplates. Between them, the eight ironmen had carried and dropped *2 million pounds* of rails.

Crocker won his bet, and the Central Pacific set a tracklaying record that has never been beaten.

THE GOLDEN SPIKE

The Central Pacific's tracklaying crews finished their last few miles by May 1, when Strobridge ordered his work gangs back from the end of the line. Union Pacific crews finished their grading to Promontory on May 7; they were also pulled back, as Promontory Summit itself lacked enough water to support a camp of several thousand people. Two engines approached Promontory from east and west of the final meeting point: Union Pacific engine No. 119, and Central Pacific No. 60, the *Jupiter.*

Plans for the meeting ceremony went forward despite some last-minute trouble. With the end of construction in sight, the railroads began laying off their workers, and fighting, gambling, and killing went on for days in the work camps. The violence spread to nearby Mormon farms and towns. An argument among Chinese workers over a gambling debt turned into a long melee at a camp known as Victory Station. To get the situation under control, both railroads hurried workers away from Promontory, while the Union Pacific handed out free passes to now-unemployed laborers for the trip back to Omaha.

The directors of the Union Pacific traveling west for the joining ceremony encountered bad weather on May 7. Rainfall and snowmelt in Weber Canyon caused torrential floods, weakening the bridge at Devil's Gate, the trestle at Strawberry Ford, and the bridge at Slate Point so dangerously that trains could no longer cross them. The floods also washed out several miles of grades along the route. Crews repaired the grades and shored up the bridge spans with wood hurried down from the Union Pacific's supply depots. Unable to pass through Weber Canyon, Dodge, Durant, and Sidney Dillon supervised the repair work themselves.

The ceremonial "Lincoln" car, which was carrying the Union Pacific officers, had been held up behind the Devil's Gate bridge. As a matter of pride, Durant and Dillon did not want to cross the canyon on horseback. If they did so, they would be forced to use an ordinary passenger car while their Central Pacific rivals enjoyed their own mahogany-lined, brass-fitted Presidential Special palace car. Durant and Dillon waited for the

ON THE CURIOUS KIDNAPPING OF THOMAS DURANT

There was considerable trouble among Union Pacific workers in the spring of 1869. Many of them had not been paid for months, and bitter resentment was building. When tie cutters and graders working for contractor James W. Davis realized that Thomas Durant himself would soon be coming through for the joining ceremony at Promontory, they decided to take action.

Charles Edgar Ames, in his book *Pioneering the Union Pacific,* describes the situation as Durant's train pulled into the station at Piedmont, Wyoming.

> Like a bolt from the blue rifles blazed, and the engine was stopped by ties piled on the track. A mob of some 300 armed men, all tie-cutters and graders on the UP, was waiting outside. Uncoupling the official car and waving the train onward, they swarmed around Durant. The spokesmen angrily demanded their back pay, overdue for months. They would hold Durant and Duff there until it was paid. The sum was said to be something like $200,000 or even more. Durant had no such amount, of course, but quietly assuring his captors that he was in full sympathy with their plight, he telegraphed Oliver Ames in Boston to send the money. Oliver flashed a wire to Dodge to send the troops instead. Dodge ordered up a company of infantry from the nearest army post at Fort Bridger. But [Sydney] Dillon, who had been appealed to by Dodge, for some unknown reason ordered the troop train not to stop at Piedmont. The kidnappers then wired Dodge to put up the money within 24 hours, or else.

Finally the company's officers wired the money, and Durant was released by his angry captors—or so the story goes. A very suspicious Grenville Dodge suspected Thomas Durant of faking his own kidnapping, in order to force his partners to pay the late wages out of their own pockets. Nor was Oliver Ames, who finally authorized the release of the money, so sure of Durant's plight. Charles Edgar Ames's book quotes him as follows:

> I am informed that Davis & Associate men were the parties stopping the train. Could it be one of Durant's plans to have these men get their pay out of the Road and we suffer for his benefit? Durant is so strange a man that I am prepared to believe any sort of rascality that may be charged against him.

bridge at Devil's Gate to become passable again, delaying the ceremony another day.

The honorary Central Pacific train had arrived from Sacramento on May 6 with Leland Stanford, William Sherman, and Arizona governor A. P. K. Stafford aboard. The train also carried several important souvenirs for the coming ceremony. Contractor David Hewes had fashioned a spike out of melted-down gold coins, its four sides engraved with the names of the Central Pacific directors. (The San Francisco *News Letter* supplied a second gold spike.) A tie contractor fashioned a ceremonial last tie out of polished laurel wood that carried silver bands and an engraved ceremonial plaque. A silver spike arrived from Virginia City, Nevada, and the Arizona Territory sent a spike of silver, gold, and iron.

A grand ceremony was prepared in Sacramento, where twenty-five trainloads of celebrants arrived. The party had been scheduled for May 8; when news reached Sacramento that the joining ceremony had been delayed, the

With the driving of these ceremonial spikes, the transcontinental railroad was completed.

festivities went ahead anyway. At 10:00 A.M. on Saturday, May 8, the brass cannon "Union Boy" thundered, shots rang out, bells were rung, and two dozen locomotives set off their whistles.

That night, the Lincoln car moved up to the Devil's Gate bridge at a crawl, with men walking ahead to check the grade and the bridge. The conductor refused to let the engineer cross the bridge at night, prompting many passengers to leave the train and take wagons down into Salt Lake. On Sunday, May 9, the train finally got through. On the same day at Promontory, workers put down the last ties and laid the two final rails under a tarpaulin.

As described by Hubert Howe Bancroft,

The spot where the joining of the Atlantic to the Pacific took place was a grassy plain sunken between green hills . . . in the immediate vicinity were a few canvas

tents. Moving about the ground, mingling in a pictur-
esque confusion, were people from the Occident and the
Orient—Mongolian, Celt, full-blooded aborigine, and
half-caste Mexican, garbed in national costumes, or in-
nocent of any, mixing freely with American citizens.[36]

Late in the morning of Monday, May 10, about six hundred
people gathered at Promontory Summit to witness the final joining of the transcontinental railroad. As the crowds milled about
the two locomotives, bands that had come up from Ogden
started to play. Appearing were Durant, Sidney Dillon, Grenville
Dodge, the Casement brothers, and Samuel Reed. The rival directors shook hands. Telegraph operator W. N. Shilling prepared
to tap out bulletins that would be posted and read instantly all
over the country. Four companies of the U.S. Army's Twenty-first
Infantry Regiment lined up in double file alongside the track.

While Central Pacific and Union Pacific gangs lifted the last
rails, Strobridge and Reed carried the ceremonial laurel tie from
the Central Pacific car and laid it into place. At 12:27 prayers
were offered by the Reverend John Todd of Pittsfield, Massachusetts, and John Sharp of the Mormon Church.

The ceremonial spikes were placed into their holes in the tie.
Stanford had the first swing at the spike, but missed. Thomas
Durant then missed as well. Strobridge and Reed drove the
spikes home, while telegraph wires connected to the spike hammer transmitted the final blows. As the work was completed,
Shilling punched out the dots and dashes spelling out the last
word: "Done." The time was 12:47 P.M. One final ceremony took
place: the taking of a commemorative photograph.

> The C.P.'s "Jupiter" and the U.P.'s No. 119 eased forward
> until their pilots clanged together. While cheering work-
> men climbed up onto both Iron Horses, their engineers
> scrambled to the boiler fronts with bottles of champagne,
> to shake hands and exchange toasts. The photographers
> worked frantically to clear the crowd back so that the
> railroad's chief engineers, Grenville Dodge and Samuel
> Montague, could stand before the two locomotives in an-
> other symbolic handclasp.[37]

At that moment, a magnetic ball was dropping from the
Capitol building in Washington; the Liberty Bell was ringing in

A continent is joined! With the completion of the transcontinental railroad, a new era in travel in the United States began.

Philadelphia; and a naval battery in New York City fired a one-hundred-gun salute. Parades were under way in every major city and in hundreds of small towns.

The formal message from Promontory read as follows:

> The last rail is laid! The last spike is driven! The Pacific Railroad is completed! The point of junction is 1,086 miles west of the Missouri River, and 690 miles east of Sacramento City. Signed, Leland Stanford, Central Pacific Railroad; T. C. Durant, Sidney Dillon, John Duff, Union Pacific Railroad.[38]

THE UNITED CONTINENT

The Union Pacific and the Central Pacific had fulfilled the long-held dream of Lewis and Clark and many others: a trade highway that would link the Atlantic and Pacific Coasts, thus enabling the rapid settlement and economic development of the western United States.

Indeed, the transcontinental railroad meant something even bigger, as Lucius Beebe and Charles Clegg observed—the end of the western frontier:

THE SAD FATE OF PROMONTORY

Although it enjoyed a moment of glory in the final joining of the Union Pacific and Central Pacific, the town of Promontory soon fell on hard times. As described by Lucius Beebe and Charles Clegg in *Hear the Train Blow,*

Pullman passengers rarely disembarked at Promontory.

Promontory's economic decline . . . began with the inclusion of through Pullmans [sleeping cars] in the *Overland Express* . . . so that only the most venturesome and resolute descended from the cars to investigate the town's possibilities. Helper engines and freight crews operated out of Promontory for a time but in a few years Ogden was made the junction of the two railroads and Promontory's fortunes declined even further.

In 1905 the Lucin Cutoff bridging Salt Lake was built and all important traffic routed over it at great saving of time and money; only occasional freights passed where once the engine pilots had touched head to head. During the Second World War the rails were torn up and the town itself disappeared completely.

The Old West was passing and the symbols were Dr. Durant's and President Stanford's mahogany fitted business cars, the toasts drunk in vintage French wines from silver coolers at the conclusion of the ceremonies, and the presence of news reporters and photographers with facilities for the instant transmission of intelligence to the farthest reaches of the continental empire.[39]

At first, however, the transcontinental railroad did more harm than good. Thousands of railroad laborers found themselves unemployed after the two roads joined at Promontory. The old transportation industries of stagecoach and overland wagon trains died out, throwing thousands of teamsters out of work and putting an important service industry out of business. For the Native Americans of the Great Plains, the railroad would bring the destruction of a traditional way of life. And the hope of many railroad promoters, who believed the road would make the United States a wealthy middleman in a trading network between Europe and Asia, proved to be an illusion. With the opening of the Suez Canal in Egypt later in 1869, a much shorter route between Europe and Asia came into use.

At first, the railroad's lower freight rates also forced California merchants to sell goods, transported at great expense by steamship via Panama, at a steep loss. But the railroad also brought these merchants a boom in customers because of increased population and economic activity. California farms and factories could now sell to the enormous markets east of the Rockies. Nevada mines could dig less-valuable metal ores, such as iron and copper, and ship them east for smelting. Wyoming and Colorado could ship beef and coal. Immigrants could reach the valleys of California and Oregon in a few days, claim their lands, and build their homes.

On May 15, 1869, five days after the celebration at Promontory, regular transcontinental passenger service began. It took five days, at an average speed of twenty miles an hour, to complete the trip between Sacramento and Omaha. The entire country could be spanned by trains in eight days instead of in six to eight weeks by stagecoach line. For many people, the trip west became an excursion, a pleasure trip, instead of a dangerous ordeal. For immigrants from Europe, cheap land in Nebraska and points west was there for the taking, eagerly sold by the agents of the Union Pacific.

The transcontinental railroad helped to usher in the Gilded Age, the long economic boom of the late nineteenth century. Theodore Judah's vision would be realized, and the Union Pacific and the Central Pacific would prosper. New transcontinental lines, including the Northern Pacific and the Southern Pacific, would be built within a few years of the Promontory ceremony. For more than fifty years, railroads would dominate trade and transportation in the United States, until the time that an even faster mode of travel would begin its own wheeled way across the enormous continent.

NOTES

Introduction
1. Robert Howard, *The Great Iron Trail: The Story of the First Transcontinental Railroad.* New York: Putnam, 1962, p. 99.

Chapter 1: Raising Steam
2. Oliver Jensen, *The American Heritage History of Railroads in America.* New York: Random House, 1993, p. 28.
3. Samuel Eliot Morison, *The Oxford History of the American People.* New York: Oxford University Press, 1965, p. 478.
4. James E. Vance Jr., *The North American Railroad: Its Origin, Evolution, and Geography.* Baltimore: Johns Hopkins University Press, 1995, p. 169.
5. Howard, *The Great Iron Trail,* p. 101.
6. James McCague, *Moguls and Iron Men.* New York: Harper & Row, 1964, p. 20.
7. Edwin L. Sabin, *Building the Pacific Railway.* Balboa Island, CA: Paisano Press, 1919, pp. 49–50.
8. Stewart H. Holbrook, *The Story of American Railroads.* New York: Crown, 1947, p. 165.

Chapter 2: Breaking Ground
9. Dee Brown, *Hear That Lonesome Whistle Blow: Railroads in the West.* New York: Simon & Schuster, 1977, p. 50.
10. McCague, *Moguls and Iron Men,* p. 78.
11. Oscar Lewis, *The Big Four: The Story of Huntington, Stanford, Hopkins, and Crocker, and of the Building of the Central Pacific.* New York: Knopf, 1963, pp. 68–69.
12. Wesley S. Griswold, *A Work of Giants.* New York: McGraw-Hill, 1962, p. 34.
13. Lewis, *The Big Four,* p. 46.

Chapter 3: False Starts on the Union Pacific
14. Charles Edgar Ames, *Pioneering the Union Pacific: A Reappraisal of the Builders of the Railroad.* New York: Meredith Corporation, 1969, pp. 22–23.
15. Griswold, *A Work of Giants,* p. 58.
16. Brown, *Hear That Lonesome Whistle Blow,* p. 54.
17. Quoted in Griswold, *A Work of Giants,* p. 59.
18. Morison, *The Oxford History of the American People,* pp. 730–31.

19. Quoted in Ames, *Pioneering the Union Pacific*, p. 501.

20. Brown, *Hear That Lonesome Whistle Blow*, p. 61.

21. Quoted in Brown, *Hear That Lonesome Whistle Blow*, p. 61.

Chapter 4: The Conquest of the Sierra Nevada

22. Quoted in Griswold, *A Work of Giants*, p. 121.

23. McCague, *Moguls and Iron Men*, pp. 229–30.

24. Sabin, *Building the Pacific Railway*, pp. 114–15.

25. McCague, *Moguls and Iron Men*, p. 147.

26. Quoted in Ames, *Pioneering the Union Pacific*, p. 802.

Chapter 5: Trouble on the Plains

27. Glenn Chesney Quiett, *They Built the West: An Epic of Rails and Cities*. New York: Appleton-Century Crofts, 1934, pp. 36–38.

28. Quoted in Ames, *Pioneering the Union Pacific*, p. 647.

29. Quoted in Ames, *Pioneering the Union Pacific*, p. 216.

30. John F. Stover, *American Railroads*, 2nd ed. Chicago: University of Chicago Press, 1997, p. 66.

31. William L. Withuhn, ed., *Rails Across America: A History of Railroads in North America*. New York: Smithmark Publishers, 1993, p. 31.

32. Jensen, *The American Heritage History of Railroads in America*, p. 98.

Chapter 6: Meeting at Promontory

33. Quoted in Howard, *The Great Iron Trail*, p. 321.

34. Quoted in McCague, *Moguls and Iron Men*, p. 301.

35. Howard, *The Great Iron Trail*, p. 327.

36. Quoted in Withuhn, *Rails Across America*, p. 39.

37. Brown, *Hear That Lonesome Whistle Blow*, pp. 132–33.

38. Union Pacific Railroad, *Union Pacific Railroad, a Brief History*. Omaha, NB: The Omaha Printing Company, 1946, p. 10.

39. Lucius Beebe and Charles Clegg, *Hear the Train Blow: A Pictorial Epic of America in the Railroad Age*. New York: Dutton, 1952, p. 148.

FOR FURTHER READING

John Coiley, *Train.* New York: Knopf, 1992. A book in magazine format, which uses imaginative two-page photo spreads on everything from "The First Railroads" to "Making Tracks" and "Royal Trains."

Joy Hakim, *Reconstruction and Reform.* New York: Oxford University Press, 1994. A detailed account of the post–Civil War period, taking the development of the railroads into account.

J. B. Snell, *Early Railways.* London: Octopus Books, 1972. The story of the first railways built in Great Britain, Europe, and the United States.

Patrick B. Whitehouse, ed., *World of Trains,* London: Hamlyn Publishing Group, 1976. A behind-the-scenes look at railroad operations in the United States and Europe.

Sydney Wood, *Trains and Railroads.* New York: Dorling Kindersley, 1992. Introduction to train mechanics and history using hundreds of detailed illustrations and photographs.

Bill Yenne, ed., *All Aboard: The Golden Age of American Rail Travel.* Greenwich, CT: Brompton Books, 1989. A big picture book about the golden age of rail travel in the late nineteenth and early twentieth centuries.

WORKS CONSULTED

Charles Edgar Ames, *Pioneering the Union Pacific: A Reappraisal of the Builders of the Railroad.* New York: Meredith Corporation, 1969. A long and extremely detailed book on the financing and engineering of the Union Pacific and the involvement of the Ames brothers.

Lucius Beebe and Charles Clegg, *Hear the Train Blow: A Pictorial Epic of America in the Railroad Age.* New York: Dutton, 1952. A big, old-fashioned coffee-table book illustrating the best-known tales of nineteenth-century adventures aboard the Iron Horse.

Dee Brown, *Hear That Lonesome Whistle Blow: Railroads in the West.* New York: Simon & Schuster, 1977. An anecdotal account of the conquest of the West by the Iron Horse, describing the effect it had on immigration, industrialization, urbanization, and traditional Native American societies.

George H. Douglas, *All Aboard! The Railroad in American Life.* New York: Paragon House, 1992. A book that describes the effect of the railroads on American society and communities, from settlement to suburbanization.

Sarah H. Gordon, *Passage to Union: How the Railroads Transformed American Life, 1829–1929.* Chicago: Ivan R. Dee, 1996. A skeptical recounting of railroad history that details the various scandals and shenanigans of the railroad barons and the damaging social effects of railroad development.

Wesley S. Griswold, *A Work of Giants.* New York: McGraw-Hill, 1962. A straightforward retelling of the transcontinental railroad saga.

Stewart H. Holbrook, *The Story of American Railroads.* New York: Crown, 1947. An authoritative, encyclopedic history of railroad construction, using firsthand accounts of railroad workers, engineers, and superintendents.

Robert Howard, *The Great Iron Trail: The Story of the First Transcontinental Railroad.* New York: Putnam, 1962. A book on the transcontinental railroad written in an episodic, journalistic style.

Oliver Jensen, *The American Heritage History of Railroads in America.* New York: Random House, 1993. An imaginative, absorbing volume on railroad history using surprising photographs and interesting original sources.

Oscar Lewis, *The Big Four: The Story of Huntington, Stanford, Hopkins, and Crocker, and of the Building of the Central Pacific.* New York: Knopf, 1963. Biographical sketches of the Central Pacific partners, focusing on their careers, work habits, personalities, and opinions of the railroad and of each other.

James McCague, *Moguls and Iron Men.* New York: Harper & Row, 1964. A detailed description of the Union Pacific and Central Pacific, with emphasis on the financial maneuvering that made the transcontinental railroad possible.

Samuel Eliot Morison, *The Oxford History of the American People.* New York: Oxford University Press, 1965. A comprehensive one-volume survey of American history from the first Native American settlement to the 1960s.

Glenn Chesney Quiett, *They Built the West: An Epic of Rails and Cities.* New York: Appleton-Century Crofts, 1934. A straightforward and thorough description of railroad development west of the Missouri River.

Edwin L. Sabin, *Building the Pacific Railway.* Balboa Island, CA: Paisano Press, 1919. A highly opinionated account of the railroad, interesting for its dated and extravagant prose.

John F. Stover, *American Railroads,* 2nd ed. Chicago: University of Chicago Press, 1997. An exploration of the effect of the national rail network on the U.S. economy and the railroads' relation to major events in U.S. history.

————, *The Life and Decline of the American Railroad.* New York: Oxford University Press, 1970. A scholarly review of railroad history, the decline of the railroads in the twentieth century in the face of new modes of transport, and a look at a possible future for surviving railroad companies.

Union Pacific Railroad, *Union Pacific Railroad, a Brief History.* Omaha, NB: The Omaha Printing Company, 1946. A short book with many interesting details.

James E. Vance Jr., *The North American Railroad: Its Origin, Evolution, and Geography.* Baltimore: Johns Hopkins University Press, 1995. A beautifully illustrated scientific treatise on early railroad engineering and economics in North America.

William L. Withuhn, ed., *Rails Across America: A History of Railroads in North America.* New York: Smithmark Publishers, 1993. A colorful and detailed book on railroading, using specially commissioned photographs of railroad artifacts.

INDEX

PICTURE CREDITS

ABOUT THE AUTHOR

Tom Streissguth has written more than 30 books of non-fiction for young readers, from *Life Among the Vikings* to *Utopian Visionaries; Lewis and Clark; Wounded Knee: The End of the Plains Indian Wars;* and the award-winning *Hustlers and Hoaxers.* He has written or collaborated on dozens of geography books as well as biographies and descriptive histories. His interests include music, languages, and travel. He has also co-founded a private language school, "Learn French!", which hosts summer tours each year in Europe. He lives in Florida with his wife and two daughters.